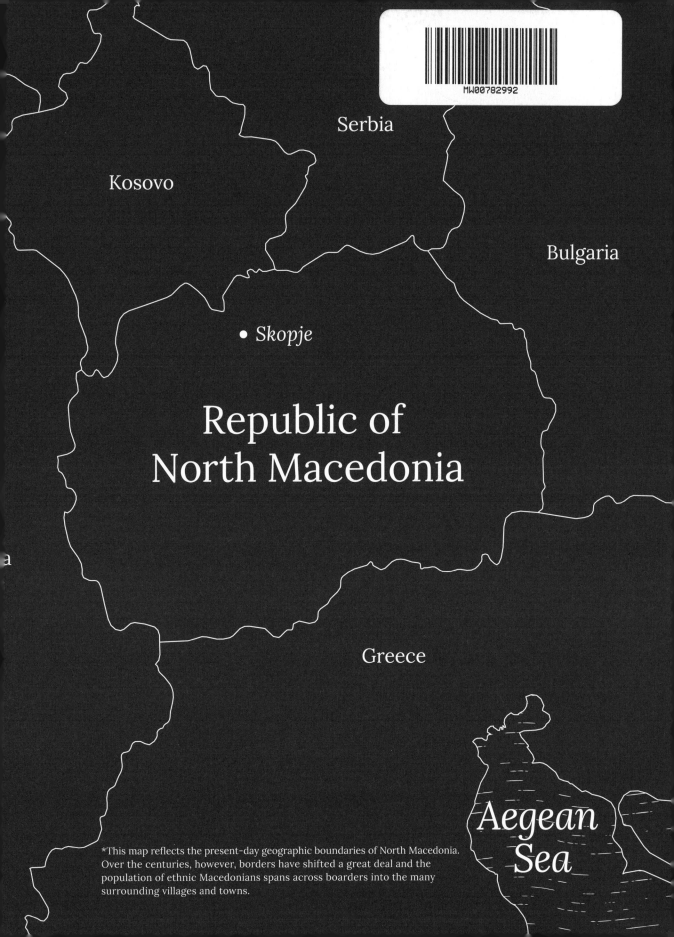

Serbia

Kosovo

Bulgaria

• *Skopje*

Republic of
North Macedonia

a

Greece

*Aegean
Sea*

*This map reflects the present-day geographic boundaries of North Macedonia.
Over the centuries, however, borders have shifted a great deal and the
population of ethnic Macedonians spans across boarders into the many
surrounding villages and towns.

MACEDONIA

THE COOKBOOK

MACEDONIA

THE COOKBOOK

KATERINA NITSOU

Photography by Oliver Fitzgerald

Interlink Books

First published in 2021 by
INTERLINK BOOKS
An imprint of Interlink Publishing Group, Inc.
46 Crosby Street
Northampton, Massachusetts 01060
www.interlinkbooks.com

Library of Congress Cataloging-in-Publication Data available
ISBN 978-1-62371-879-4

Publisher: Michel Moushabeck
Editor: Leyla Moushabeck
Designer: Harrison Williams
Proofreader: Jane Bugaeva

For our complete catalog visit our website at
www.interlinkbooks.com or e-mail:
sales@interlinkbooks.com

Printed and bound in Korea

10 9 8 7 6 5 4 3 2 1

MIX
Paper from
responsible sources
FSC® C023083

The paper in this book is FSC© certified. FSC© promotes environmentally responsible, socially beneficial, and economically viable management of the world's forests. Vegetable-based printing ink has been used throughout.

To my mother, Linda, and to my
teta Sophie for all their support
and guidance, and to Oliver whom I
could not have done this without.

CONTENTS
Sodržina

Preface 9
Introduction 11
Macedonian Culture 15

Mezze 18
Small Plates

Salata 48
Salads

Supa 76
Soups

Meso 102
Meats

Zhivina 130
Poultry

Riba 156
Fish

Zelenchuk 172
Vegetables and Side Dishes

Leb 198
Breads

Slatko 226
Sweets

Zimnica 252
Preserves

Author's Notes 268
Acknowledgments 268
Index 270

PREDGOVOR PREFACE

As a Macedonian woman, I have learned the importance of food. As a chef, I have learned how to refine that food. My maternal grandfather was a chef in his own restaurant and, among others in my family, very inspirational to my culinary career.

In the late 1920s, during the first major wave of Macedonian immigration to North America, my grandfather traveled to Canada at the age of twenty-two. His father had died when he was nine, and as the only "man" in the family, he believed he was leaving home to seek a brighter future. Little did he know he was heading straight into the Great Depression. Upon arrival, he did not speak a word of English but he was committed to making Canada his new home. In Toronto, he united with fellow Macedonians to navigate the perils of his new home, managing to survive by eating bean soup and cabbage stew.

Working odd jobs, he eventually saved enough money to open what became a very successful restaurant in the heart of downtown Toronto. He served a combination of traditional Macedonian fare and North American–style diner food. He had a wonderful ability for maximizing flavor, while maintaining the simplicity of what he was cooking.

Throughout his life and career, he didn't just cook. He developed methods and reasons for the "whys" and the "hows" of food. Although my grandfather was not formally trained, he understood his craft immensely well and certainly set a masterful standard of quality. He was meticulous when it came to cooking, and this devotion to perfection was the first lesson I learned in respecting the integrity of the ingredient.

My father's family did not leave the "old country" to move to Toronto until the 1960s. My father's two sisters moved to Toronto first, as teenagers, and my father hoped that he and his parents and younger brother would one day be reunited with them. Having studied at university in Greece, my father was able to come to Canada as a landed immigrant quite quickly. His parents and younger brother followed in 1972, and his family was able to realize its dreams of being reunited. When I was growing up, my entire extended family lived in Toronto, and it was through my father's side that I learned to enjoy large family gatherings and the cooking that went with them. The weekends and holidays of my childhood were loud and colorful, and filled with people. During these gatherings, I watched my mother, grandmother, aunts, and cousins working together in the kitchen to put together a feast—in particular, my father's sister Sophie, who was also a restaurateur in Toronto and has an incredible knowledge of the way food was prepared in the village and the appropriate protocol when it comes to which foods are to be served and for which occasions. My mother and my aunt both played integral roles in developing my love of cooking and hosting. It is something they both did so effortlessly, and which brought so much joy to our family.

I've always loved the family style of eating—the sharing of large platters around the table and the way the flavors complemented each other beautifully on the plate. The great thing about Macedonian cuisine is that regardless of what combination of dishes is being served, it all seems to work and make sense as a single, bountiful spread. I have been diligent in maintaining the true essence of Macedonian cuisine in this book. I have also updated and simplified some of the recipes so they are easy for modern home cooks to master. I began writing this book before I started my culinary training at Le Cordon Bleu where I was able to refine my techniques. My internship at the Los Angeles Times Test Kitchen, however, truly helped redefine my ability to write recipes.

I chose to write a Macedonian cookbook because it is the food I know best and the food that I love most. I also want to teach and share with others a bit about this glorious part of the world. I have always believed, as most chefs do, that the best way to learn about any country or culture is through its food and, more importantly, through its kitchens.

Through my research for this book, I realized that there is much abundance in Macedonian cuisine, much more than the few dozen recipes that were the staples in my home growing up. While writing, there were many times in my own kitchen that I felt deeply connected to my family and my ancestry simply because I was preparing food that they had been making for centuries. A celebration of a culture, this book is a journey into a culinary world that is modest, simple, and honest.

VOVED

INTRODUCTION

The food of Macedonia is rustic and unassuming, guided by the land and perfected by the people. It embodies a culinary tradition that has been deeply rooted and passed down through generations, while being inspired along the way by the surrounding cultures that have left their footprint on the region.

The people of Macedonia date back to ancient times. Before our common era, Macedonia was vast and spread over much of the southern Balkan Peninsula. So when referencing Macedonia in this book, I mean the geographic area of the Kingdom of Alexander the Great, which Macedonians inhabit. Presently the country is called North Macedonia, although for centuries Macedonians have inhabited the lands that surround the country's current border.

But food has no borders, and over many centuries, this geographic area was occupied and culturally influenced by the Byzantine Empire, the Christian Orthodox Church, the Turkish Ottoman Empire, the Balkan Wars, and the First and Second World Wars. Macedonians have inevitably assimilated some of the culinary and cultural practices, ingredients, and flavors these cultures brought with them that are now staples in the Macedonian kitchen. Most notably, they brought spices such as cinnamon and mahleb (made from the ground seeds of a sour cherry tree) from Turkey and the Middle East, rice from the Orient, and olive oil and citrus from the Mediterranean.

The cultivation of Macedonian cuisine has evolved over thousands of years as a reaction to what grew locally, as well as to trade that was taking place. Even though borders have changed drastically over the last two thousand years, the spirit and heart of the Macedonian people still pulses among the rolling mountains and valleys. With Serbia and Kosovo to the North, Bulgaria to the East, Greece to the South and Albania to the West, Macedonia remains well regarded as a center for agriculture among its neighboring countries. There are cultural crossovers, not only between the surrounding countries but also from the neighboring villages and towns.

The terrain of Macedonia is undulating. Colorful fruits and vegetables grow in the mountains and valleys; livestock and freshwater fish are abundant. With micro-growing conditions within Macedonia and a long history of rudimentary farming practices, the groundwork was set for the cuisine to be highly adaptable to whatever grew well and in abundance that year. The origins of our recipes are quite ancient, yet continue to flourish and are still staples today. Our dishes have been perfected in Macedonian homes for centuries and passed down from generation to generation, each family or region taking a slightly different approach. Luckily, it is not an overly complicated way to cook. There are no special tools or procedures that are necessary to accomplish these dishes. The goal of each dish is to simply achieve balance, and to highlight the quality and integrity of the ingredients.

Today, Macedonia's landscape still remains quite rustic and rural, with much of its industry focused on agriculture. The rich fertile land, sunshine, and temperate climate makes agriculture a necessary and natural choice. The selection of the fruits, vegetables, and herbs grown in the countryside are bountiful and robust with flavor. Macedonia is also known for its quality of grapes, which makes for award-winning wines that are now beginning to receive global acclaim. Wine history in Macedonia can be traced back to around 1300 BC, at least 700 years before grapevine origins in France. Rakija is also a very popular fruit spirit that can be made with plums or apricots, but in Macedonia it is typically made with white grapes and anise. Peppers are perhaps one of the most popular ingredients in Macedonia, with a multitude of varieties, but most notably the heirloom Rezha Macedonian pepper. They are incorporated into many of the recipes, or simply roasted with oil, garlic, and salt and enjoyed as a standard accompaniment to meals. Ajvar (page 27), a dip made with roasted peppers, is another national specialty. Beans play a huge role in the canvas of the Macedonian cuisine and are highly regarded for their quality. Tavche Gravche (Traditional White Bean Stew, page 177) is Macedonia's national dish.

Many of the Macedonians I know and grew up with are from rural villages. My father's village is called Rula, and my mother's village is Bresnitza. Both are within the Lerin (Florina) region of present-day northern Greece. In the last century, my family, along with thousands of other Macedonians, emigrated to countries like Canada, Australia, and the United States. I was born and raised in Toronto, and although I did not grow up in Macedonia, Macedonian culture was very prevalent in my own life and upbringing. Macedonian was my first spoken language, and our social interactions as children were shared with our very large extended family who all held the memories of their motherland dear to their hearts. This love of culture was imparted to us as children through dance, art, music—and of course, food. True to the adaptative nature of the cuisine, we were brought up with traditional Macedonian food that was altered to utilize what was available in North America. Instead of the Rezha pepper, we used red bell peppers or banana peppers. Hospitality and family gatherings were at the core of our childhood, and through this, we learned about our traditions. Overall, our culture is quite social, and the gathering of people is a big part of daily life. These gatherings were never formal. They were open to all, and the ethos was always, "Whatever we have, we will share it with you." This way of thinking made gatherings pleasurable because there was no pressure to make hosting complicated.

Macedonian cities and villages are filled with flourishing markets, bustling street cafes, and restaurants with large patios that spill out onto the street. Macedonians love going out for a rashetka (outing) to have a drink and snack at a kafeana (café) and to listen to music and socialize. Religious and nonreligious festivals are also popular in the cities and villages. Huge gatherings of people celebrate with live music, dancing, food, and drinks. Growing up in Toronto, we celebrated the same way. There would be winter dances and summer picnics nearly every weekend. These were big events, often with hundreds of people attending.

Yet to sample the true essence of Macedonian culture, one must dig deep into the home, where you capture the authenticity of the food and the stories of the Macedonian people. Home is where men and women come together to enjoy the fruits of their labors through the recipes that have been handed down and perfected over many generations. Capturing this was at the heart of creating this book.

MACEDONIAN CULTURE

The Macedonian culture is rich and deeply rooted in tradition with a charming tapestry of music, dance, dress, celebrations, rituals, and food. With so many different cities and villages, it is only natural that there are different approaches and variances to the customs and traditions. Each city or village collectively shared in the same core traditions but often with slightly different approaches.

My interpretation of the culture is based on the small villages my parents are from. Even though they were neighboring villages and only about six kilometers away from each other, there were quite distinct differences in their dialect, way of dressing, and technical skill sets. For example, my mother's village was a little more modern and the common trade was stone masonry, whereas my father's village was much more agriculturally guided. The majority of Macedonians are Christian Orthodox. Although there are many other religions being practiced, Orthodox Christianity remains the main religion of Macedonians. I touch on this because religious celebrations are deeply woven throughout the culture. Weddings, births, baptisms, and funerals are milestones in many cultures and specific foods are prepared for each. For example, at weddings a very large ornate round bread called Pogacha (Braided Rich Bread, page 202) is made and decorated with braided dough and sesame seeds. After the ceremony, the bride and groom each hold one end of the bread and tear it apart. Whoever tears off the largest piece is meant to "rule the household." The bread is then portioned out and each guest at the wedding must have a piece for good luck.

In the Christian Orthodox tradition, there are saints' name days, which celebrate the feast days of different saints. Babies were often named after a saint, and their saint's name day is celebrated similarly to a birthday. It is a big celebration, and for Macedonians, name days are much anticipated annual events. The day is typically celebrated in the home and an offering of Kozinak (Easter Bread, page 206) and pchenica (sweet wheat berries) along with cookies, cakes, and red wine are given to visiting guests and family. "Srekna Slava" or "Sreken Imenden"—salutations meaning "Happy Saint Day" or "Happy Name Day"—are shared for good luck.

Macedonians can also be quite superstitious. Because superstitions are the storytelling and the legacy of every civilization, many superstitions have survived in Macedonia and are still believed in today. They may vary from family to family and city to city, but whether believed in or not, they provide insight into the Macedonian way of life. One of the superstitions from my mother's village was that it was considered very bad luck, and an act of greed, to be holding food in both hands at the same time during meals. Another that many believe in is the "evil eye." My grandmother was really adamant about covering babies with loose muslin when in public so strangers couldn't see them. She also believed in putting a bit of salt on babies' tongues to protect them from the "evil eye." Superstitions in Macedonia run deep—an entire book could be devoted to this topic alone!

Traditional Macedonian music dates back centuries, and it was highly influenced by the Ottoman Empire. It is folk music that over the years took on Oriental elements to create a distinct sound. Macedonian folk music is heavily vocal and created by a small band of musicians that play instruments like a gaida, which is similar to a Scottish bagpipe, a tapan, which is a double-headed bass drum, a tambura, a stringed instrument like a mandolin, and a kaval, which is like a large flute. As the music modernized, key instruments in Macedonian music now include the clarinet, guitar, and traditional drums. Currently, there is a new generation of young Macedonian artists who are creating pop and rock music, but there is still a deep love for the traditional folk music, even among younger generations. Younger artists are also incorporating the traditional folk songs, as well as new lyrics, into their own melodies. The repertoire of Macedonian music is very expressive, as it touches on all aspects of human experience, including love, family, loss, war, and playful humor.

Much of the music is upbeat and suitable for dancing. With the traditional music, there are specific dances that correspond to each song. Traditional Macedonian dancing involves quite intricate footwork, where people hold hands and dance in a counterclockwise circle, called an oro. One of Macedonia's most popular songs is "Makedonsko Devojče," written and composed by Jonče Hristovski in 1964 about a Macedonian maiden and her beauty. Truly beautiful, it is a popular choice for the bride's oro at her wedding. At Macedonian weddings, each family member is honored with an oro that they get to choose and lead, as a sign of respect to that person.

Another popular Macedonian custom at weddings is the bieshetoe oro, "pig dance," which is performed at the reception. In this dance, members of the wedding party arrive with bottles of wine and carrying a beautiful roasted suckling pig. They bring the pig to the future godparents (best man and maid of honor) and tauntingly "demand" payment for the pig. The godparents adorn the platter with money, and the pig is then taken and portioned for all the guests. The money goes to the happy couple as a sign of good fortune and prosperity for their future. This custom is always performed with the theme of festivity and joy, as the guests clap along.

Traditional Macedonian dress is another way you can see the distinct differences between villages and regions. Clothing was handmade, mainly from cotton and wool.

Bright in color, it was quite elaborate in decoration, embellished with sequins, embroidery, and coins. Women would wear a cotton or linen tunic, usually white or ivory. A woolen sleeveless overcoat would be worn over the tunic, something like a long vest that would tie in the front, and a woolen apron would be worn over that. Other items, like sleeves and high socks, would be added on in the colder months, and all would be beautifully decorated. Women typically wore a schamia, or scarf, around their heads, which would be tied behind the head for younger girls, or under the chin for older women. The men's attire was a little less elaborate but also included a tunic, along with fitted pants and, depending on the region of Macedonia, a skirt over the top of the pants and either a vest or jacket. Both women and men wore pinci, shoes made from pig's hide.

When I was a young girl, my grandmother gave me a traditional outfit from my father's village that she had made. She made one for all of her granddaughters from the original fabrics she had loomed in the village, and also before she passed away she gave me a child's dress for my daughter Kalina.

Macedonian culture is as rich as it is diverse. It is an ancient civilization that has endured centuries of conquest and war, yet Macedonians are lighthearted, joyful, and generous people who take great pride in their roots. Strong cultural ties and traditions have been practiced for centuries and are still embraced today.

MEZZE
Small Plates

Spicy Peppers 23
Luti Piperki

Olives 24
Maslinki

Roasted Red Pepper & Eggplant Dip 27
Ajvar

Roasted Eggplant Dip 29
Pindjur

Yogurt with Garlic, 31
Cucumber & Dill
Kisolo Mleko So Pechen Luk

Garlic & Walnut Dip 32
Luk I Orev Sos

Grilled Sausage Skewers 35
Lukanki

Zucchini Fritters 37
Pitulitsi So Zeleni Tikvichki

Roasted Pepper & Feta Cheese Dip 38
Piperki So Ovchjo Serenje

Bite-Size Meatballs 41
Koftinka

Stuffed Grape Leaves 42
Sarmi So Lozov List

Fried Smelts 44
Przheni Tsironi

Leek Crêpes 47
Palachinki So Praz

MEZZE
Small Plates

In the Macedonian culture, mezze is the first offering. It usually involves a combination of small tastes to enjoy at your leisure. It could be as simple as cheese, olives, and bread, or a more elaborate spread of small nibbles that pair well with alcoholic or non-alcoholic drinks. Sometimes, for casual gatherings or a light lunch, traditional mezze is all you need. A selection of a few small dishes, a glass of wine, and great conversation is my favorite way to eat and entertain.

LUTI PIPERKI

SPICY PEPPERS

Roasted peppers are the at the core of Macedonian cuisine and the first thing that comes to mind when I think of Macedonian food. They appeared on our table alongside nearly every meal. Although this recipe calls for spicy peppers, it can also be made with sweet peppers of any variety that you find in your grocery store or market.

8–10 whole hot
  banana peppers
1 teaspoon extra-virgin
  olive oil
1 garlic clove, very finely sliced
1 teaspoon chopped parsley
½ teaspoon kosher salt

Roast the peppers over a charcoal grill or a gas flame until the skins are completely charred and blistered. Alternatively broil them in the oven (directly on the rack, or on a baking sheet lined with parchment paper), rotating them every 15 minutes until charred, 30 to 45 minutes.

Place peppers in a paper bag or heatproof container. Seal and set aside for 20 minutes until cool.

Peel off the skins, keeping the stems and seeds intact.

In a large bowl, gently toss the peppers with the oil, garlic, parsley, and salt.

Arrange on a serving dish.

MASLINKI
OLIVES

Olives are a popular mezze. Although they don't commonly grow in the Macedonian region, they have become a staple in the cuisine. For guests, I love to spice up my olives right before serving them. Slightly roasting them warms the natural oils and softens their flavor.

2 lb (900 g) unpitted mixed olives stored in oil, drained

1 tablespoon extra-virgin olive oil

2 garlic cloves, finely minced

2 teaspoons lemon zest

1 teaspoon finely chopped fresh dill

½ teaspoon freshly ground black pepper

Preheat the oven to 450°F (230°C).

Rinse the olives under cold running water. Drain and pat them dry.

Arrange the olives on a baking sheet in a single layer and roast for 10 to 15 minutes until sizzling.

In a medium bowl, toss together the olive oil, garlic, lemon zest, dill, and black pepper to make a marinade.

Toss the hot olives in the marinade and stir to coat them evenly.

Let cool slightly before serving.

AJVAR
ROASTED RED PEPPER & EGGPLANT DIP

Ajvar is popular throughout the Balkans, often served as a condiment for grilled meats, or simply with bread and cheese. Macedonians take their Ajvar very seriously. In the fall, when red peppers are in season in the region, families get together outdoors with dozens of pounds of peppers to make enough jars of Ajvar for the winter months to come. It is quite labor intensive, and the work is typically rewarded with a meal of grilled sausages at the end of the day. Ajvar is made by roasting the peppers and eggplant over open flames and, traditionally, grinding them by hand, but using a food processor is much easier.

1 medium eggplant
6 red bell peppers
¼ cup (60 ml) extra-virgin
  olive oil
1 medium onion, chopped
3 garlic cloves, finely chopped
½ teaspoon crushed red
  pepper flakes
1 tablespoon red
  wine vinegar
Juice of 1 lemon
½ teaspoon white sugar
1½ teaspoons kosher salt
½ tablespoon freshly ground
  black pepper

Using a fork, pierce the eggplant skin a few times all around.

Roast the peppers and eggplant over a charcoal grill or a gas flame until the skins are completely charred and blistered. Alternatively broil them in the oven (directly on the rack or on a baking sheet lined with parchment paper), rotating every 15 minutes until charred, 30 to 45 minutes.

Place the roasted vegetables into a paper bag or a heatproof container. Seal and set aside for 20 minutes until cool.

Peel off and discard the skin and stems from the eggplant and peppers, and remove the pepper seeds. Coarsely chop the flesh and set aside.

In a large stockpot, heat the oil over medium heat and sauté the onion until very soft, about 4 minutes. Add the garlic and red pepper flakes and cook, stirring constantly, for 2 more minutes. Remove from the heat.

Add the vinegar, lemon juice, sugar, salt, and black pepper to the pot, and stir in the pepper and eggplant pulp.

Using an immersion blender or food processor, blend the mixture to a coarse paste with a slightly chunky texture. Be careful not to completely purée the mixture. Store in a glass container in the refrigerator.

PINDJUR
ROASTED EGGPLANT DIP

Pindjur is similar to Ajvar (Roasted Red Pepper and Eggplant Dip, page 27) in how it is made. These recipes were important in Macedonian homes to maximize the harvest and preserve the ingredients that were in abundance. Even growing up in Toronto, my entire family had lush, abundant gardens in their backyards and we would get together in the fall to preserve what was grown. We always had jars of Pindjur and Ajvar stored in the fridge. Both dips are delicious served as a condiment to grilled meats, or simply with cheese, olives, and toasted flatbread.

2 large eggplants
¼ yellow onion, very finely grated or minced
½ garlic clove, grated
Juice of ½ lemon
2 teaspoons kosher salt
¼ cup (60 ml) extra-virgin olive oil

Using a fork, pierce the eggplant skin a few times.

Roast the eggplants over a charcoal grill or a gas flame until skins are completely charred and blistered. Alternatively, preheat the oven to 450°F (230°C) and roast the eggplants on a baking sheet lined with parchment paper, rotating every 15 minutes until charred, 30 to 45 minutes.

Meanwhile, in a small bowl, mix together the onion, garlic, lemon juice, and salt. Cover and refrigerate for 20 minutes for the flavors to meld.

Place the roasted eggplants in a paper bag or heatproof container. Seal and set aside for 20 minutes until cool.

Remove the skins and stems, and coarsely chop the eggplant flesh. Transfer to a food processor and add the onion mixture.

With the food processor running, slowly pour in the oil. Purée until smooth.

Transfer to a dish and refrigerate for at least 2 hours before serving.

KISOLO MLEKO SO PECHEN LUK

YOGURT WITH GARLIC, CUCUMBER & DILL

Roasting the garlic is not traditional for this dip but, as a child, I always found the raw garlic to be too pungent. My family believes that garlic cures all, so they amped it up any chance they could. I found that roasting the garlic and adding a little sour cream gives this dip richness and a mild, but well-rounded flavor. It is a wonderful accompaniment to grilled meats, and I also love it with Pitulitsi So Zeleni Tikvichki (Zucchini Fritters, page 37).

1 whole garlic bulb, unpeeled

1½ teaspoons extra-virgin olive oil, divided

1½ teaspoons kosher salt, divided

½ seedless English cucumber, unpeeled, grated

1 cup (240 ml) plain full-fat Balkan yogurt (or any plain full-fat yogurt)

1 cup (240 ml) full-fat sour cream

1 tablespoon coarsely chopped fresh dill

Juice of ½ lemon

Preheat the oven to 350°F (180°C).

Cut about ½ inch (1 cm) off the top of the garlic bulb. Drizzle the cloves with ½ teaspoon of the olive oil and sprinkle with ½ teaspoon of the salt. Place the bulb in the center of a small sheet of foil and wrap it completely. Bake for 35 minutes, until soft. Remove from the oven and let cool.

Place the grated cucumber in a clean tea towel and squeeze out as much liquid as possible.

In a large mixing bowl, combine the yogurt, sour cream, 1 teaspoon olive oil, 1 teaspoon kosher salt, and the cucumber and dill.

Squeeze out the roasted garlic cloves onto a chopping board and use the back of a fork to mash the garlic to a paste. Add the mashed garlic to yogurt mixture. Add the lemon juice and stir to incorporate.

Transfer to a dish and refrigerate for at least 2 hours before serving.

LUK I OREV SOS

GARLIC & WALNUT DIP

Walnuts grow in abundance in many regions of Macedonia. Growing up, we always kept a big bucket of whole walnuts in their shells in a dark cupboard. My mother would make this recipe in a pinch if she needed something to offer to unexpected guests. We usually serve it with freshly made Pita Na Skara (Grilled Flatbread, page 211). This dish is also a great way to use up day-old bread.

5 garlic cloves, coarsely chopped

2 tablespoons red wine vinegar

1 tablespoon kosher salt

½ cup (60 g) chopped walnuts

1 lb (450 g) day-old white bread, crusts removed, coarsely chopped (about 6 cups)

½ cup (120 ml) extra-virgin olive oil, plus extra for serving

In a food processor, blend the garlic, vinegar, and salt to a paste. Use a spatula to scrape down the sides. Add the walnuts and pulse until the mixture becomes mealy (be careful not to over-process).

Place the bread in a colander in the sink and pour about 2 cups (480 ml) of hot water over it. Using your hands, squeeze out any excess water from the bread and transfer it to the food processor.

With the machine running, slowly pour in the oil. Purée until creamy.

Transfer the dip to a dish and refrigerate for at least 2 hours, before serving with a drizzle of olive oil.

LUKANKI
GRILLED SAUSAGE SKEWERS

Whenever we had company over, we served sausages. My father would head out early Saturday mornings to pick up fresh sausages from a friend who made them. There is nothing better than freshly made sausages, and we looked forward to them all day. My mother would poach them early in the day so they could be grilled just as guests were arriving. You will need 12 metal skewers or pre-soaked bamboo skewers for this dish (soak bamboo skewers for 20 minutes).

4-6 mild or spicy
Italian-style sausages

2 medium yellow onions,
cut into wedges

2 red bell peppers, cut into
bite-size pieces

1 tablespoon extra-virgin
olive oil

½ teaspoon kosher salt

Juice of ½ lemon

Using a fork, prick each sausage about 3 times on each side.

Fill a medium stockpot with warm water, add the sausages, and bring to a gentle simmer over medium heat. Let the sausages poach for 10 minutes. Drain the sausages and allow to cool.

Place the onions and peppers in a large bowl. Drizzle with the olive oil and sprinkle with the salt. Toss to coat.

Diagonally slice the sausages into 1-inch (2.5 cm) pieces.

Preheat your grill or a stovetop grill pan to medium-high heat.

Thread the sausage pieces onto skewers, alternating them with the onion and pepper pieces, making sure you have at least 2 pieces of each ingredient on each skewer.

Grill the skewers for about 5 minutes on each side or until the sausages brown and the onion and peppers are tender and nicely charred.

Transfer to a serving dish and drizzle with lemon juice. Serve immediately.

PITULITSI SO ZELENI TIKVICHKI

ZUCCHINI FRITTERS

This recipe is something we make on lazy weekend afternoons and is one of my husband's favorites. The addition of feta adds a bit of salty sharpness to the mild zucchini. Serve them with Kisolo Mleko So Pechen Luk (Yogurt with Garlic, Cucumber, and Dill, page 31) on the side.

1 lb 5 oz (600 g) zucchini (3 medium), grated

1 medium starchy potato, such as russet, peeled and grated

4 scallions, thinly sliced

¾ cup (115 g) grated feta cheese

⅓ cup (40 g) all-purpose flour

2 teaspoons finely chopped fresh dill

¼ teaspoon paprika

1 tablespoon kosher salt

½ teaspoon freshly ground black pepper

2 eggs, whisked

Vegetable oil, for frying

In a large mixing bowl, combine the zucchini, potato, scallions, and cheese.

In a separate small bowl, whisk together the flour, dill, paprika, salt, and black pepper.

Sprinkle the dry ingredients over the zucchini mixture and toss to coat. Fold the eggs into the zucchini mixture until fully incorporated.

In a large sauté pan, heat 2 tablespoons of vegetable oil until it begins to shimmer.

Without crowding the pan, drop large spoonfuls of zucchini mixture into the oil and gently press down with the back of the spoon to flatten. Fry the fritters for 5 to 6 minutes on each side until golden brown, then transfer to a plate lined with paper towels to drain excess oil. Repeat with the remaining zucchini mixture, adding about 2 tablespoons of vegetable oil to the pan for each batch. Serve immediately.

PIPERKI SO OVCHJO
ROASTED PEPPER & FETA CHEESE DIP
SERENJE

This dip is so addictive. Slightly spicy, salty, and somewhat sweet all in one. I have been a little conservative with the amount of red chili pepper flakes in this recipe but feel free to add more if you like it spicier. This dip is great alongside grilled meat dishes, but served with a loaf of bread, it can be a complete meal as it is.

MACEDONIA

38

8 red bell peppers

1 cup (150 g) grated feta cheese

1 tablespoon extra-virgin olive oil

1 teaspoon freshly squeezed lemon juice

½ teaspoon crushed red pepper flakes

1 teaspoon kosher salt

1 teaspoon freshly ground black pepper

Roast the peppers over a charcoal grill or a gas flame until the skins are completely charred and blistered. Alternatively broil them in the oven (directly on the rack, or on a baking sheet lined with parchment paper), rotating them every 15 minutes until charred, 30 to 45 minutes.

Place the roasted peppers in a paper bag or heatproof container. Seal and set aside for 20 minutes until cool.

Peel off the skins and remove the stems and seeds.

Transfer the peppers to a food processor and pulse a few times to break them up. Add the feta cheese, oil, lemon juice, red pepper flakes, salt, and black pepper. Pulse until the mixture starts to become creamy, leaving some texture.

Chill before serving.

KOFTINKA
BITE-SIZE MEATBALLS

This is my father's secret recipe. The milk makes the meat really tender and the mint adds freshness. Now that I live away from home, whenever I travel back to visit, these are always on my list of foods I want my father to make upon my arrival. They are delicious served with fresh bread and a selection of dips, like Kisolo Mleko So Pechen Luk (Yogurt with Garlic, Cucumber, and Dill, page 31), Ajvar (Roasted Red Pepper and Eggplant Dip, page 27), and Piperki So Ovchjo Serenje (Roasted Pepper and Feta Cheese Dip, page 38).

1 lb (450 g) lean ground beef

½ cup (60 g) dried breadcrumbs

4 scallions, thinly sliced

2 eggs, whisked

¼ cup (60 ml) whole milk

1½ teaspoons kosher salt

1 teaspoon freshly ground black pepper

2 tablespoons finely chopped fresh mint

1 tablespoon extra-virgin olive oil, plus extra for greasing

Preheat the oven to 450°F (230°C) and grease a baking sheet with olive oil.

In a large bowl, gently mix all of the ingredients until evenly incorporated. Be careful not to overwork the meat.

Roll the meat mixture into small balls, about 1 inch (2.5 cm) in diameter.

Arrange the meatballs on the greased baking sheet and roast for 20 to 25 minutes until cooked through.

Remove from the oven and transfer the meatballs to a plate lined with paper towels to drain excess fat.

Arrange on a serving dish.

SARMI SO

STUFFED GRAPE LEAVES

LOZOV LIST

This recipe may seem a little intimidating but it is actually quite easy. Sarmi make fantastic leftovers. My mother always doubled the recipe so we had them on hand in the fridge. I now use jarred grape leaves, but growing up, we used fresh grape vine leaves from my grandmother's garden. (If you are lucky enough to have access to fresh grape leaves, soak them in boiling salted water for about a minute to soften them before using.)

1 lb (450 g) jar of grape leaves
Boiling water
Juice of ½ lemon

In a large stockpot, bring 8 cups (2 liters) of water to a boil. Carefully remove the leaves from the jar and place them in the boiling water. Simmer for 2 minutes. Carefully remove the leaves using tongs and drain. Set aside.

FILLING

In a large bowl, gently combine the filling ingredients.

2 lb (900 g) lean ground beef
½ lb (225 g) ground pork
1 teaspoon extra-virgin
   olive oil
1 medium yellow
   onion, grated
1 egg
1 cup (240 ml) low-sodium
   chicken stock
1 tablespoon finely chopped
   fresh dill
½ teaspoon paprika
½ cup (90 g) long-grain
   white rice
2 teaspoons kosher salt
1 teaspoon freshly ground
   black pepper

Line the bottom of a stockpot with 4 or 5 leaves, overlapping them to create a base. This is a good way to use torn leaves. Place one leaf on your work surface, smooth side down. Trim the stem off at the base of the leaf and place about a tablespoonful of filling just above it. Fold each side of the leaf over the filling, and roll from the bottom to make a roll tight enough that it is secure, but not so tight that it will tear when the rice cooks. Repeat until all the filling has been used.

Arrange the stuffed grape leaves close together in the bottom of the pot in concentric circles, stacking them if needed. Pour in just enough boiling water to submerge the rolls. Squeeze in the lemon juice and place a smaller heatproof plate or pot lid on top of the rolls in the pot, to provide a gentle weight so they do not unravel during cooking. Simmer, covered, over medium-low heat, for 1 hour or until the rice is cooked.

Remove from the heat and let stand for an additional 10 minutes, covered. Carefully remove each roll and place on a baking sheet with a rack in order to drain any excess liquid. Serve warm or cold.

PRZHENI TSIRONI

FRIED SMELTS

Nothing says summer for me like freshly fried smelts. I have memories of sitting in the summer sun with my father and uncles, playing chess or cards, and snacking on these crisp little fish with a cold beer. I love the light crust you get from the flour and seasoning; this simple treatment means you can really taste the delicate fish. I prefer the mild flavor of smelts for this recipe, but if you cannot find them, you can use sardines or herring.

24 fresh or thawed smelts (12 oz/340 g), fins trimmed, and gills, head, and innards removed

½ cup (60 g) all-purpose flour

2 teaspoons kosher salt

1 teaspoon freshly ground black pepper

2 teaspoons paprika

¼ cup (60 ml) vegetable oil

1 tablespoon coarsely chopped fresh parsley

1 lemon, cut into wedges, for serving

Rinse the smelts and pat them dry.

In a shallow baking dish, mix together the flour, salt, black pepper, and paprika. Coat each fish in flour mixture.

In a large sauté pan, heat the oil until it begins to shimmer and reaches a temperature of about 350°F (180°C).

Place the smelts into oil one at a time, being careful not to overcrowd the pan. Fry the fish for 2 to 4 minutes on each side to develop a golden crust. You may need to fry in batches.

Using a slotted spoon, transfer the cooked fish to a plate lined with paper towels to drain excess oil.

Garnish with chopped parsley and lemon wedges. Serve immediately.

PALACHINKI SO PRAZ

LEEK CRÊPES

This is such an impressive dish to serve to guests. My aunt Niki would often make it for us when we visited, and it was much anticipated. As a child, it was almost like having a slice of cake, but savory. The combination of sautéed leeks, feta, and ricotta is a delicious contrast to the subtly flavored crêpes.

CRÊPES

1 cup (125 g) all-purpose flour
2 eggs
½ cup (120 ml) whole milk
1 cup (240 ml) water
½ teaspoon kosher salt
1 tablespoon unsalted butter, melted, plus extra for greasing

FILLING

1 tablespoon extra-virgin olive oil
2 large leeks (white and light green parts only), diced
1 garlic clove, minced
1 cup (240 g) ricotta cheese
1 cup (150 g) grated feta cheese
½ cup (120 ml) hot water
1 teaspoon kosher salt

In a blender, combine all of the crêpe ingredients and blend for 10 seconds until smooth. Chill in the refrigerator for 30 minutes.

Meanwhile, make the filling: In a large sauté pan, heat the olive oil over medium heat. Add the leeks and garlic and sauté until softened, 3 to 4 minutes. Remove from the heat and transfer to a mixing bowl. Whisk in the cheeses, hot water, and salt to form a paste. Set aside.

To make the crêpes: Heat a nonstick frying pan over medium heat and lightly grease with butter. Pour in just enough batter to cover the bottom of the pan and rotate the pan to form a thin layer of batter across the base. Cook until the batter becomes dry on top and the edges separate from the pan, 2 to 4 minutes. Using a spatula, gently peel away the edges and flip the crêpe over. Cook the other side for an additional 2 to 4 minutes, then transfer to a plate. Re-grease the pan with butter if needed and repeat until all of the batter has been used. You should have 6 to 8 crêpes.

Place a crêpe on a flat serving plate. Smear a large spoonful of filling (about ¼ cup/60 ml) over the surface of the crêpe, then top with another crêpe. Repeat the layering process until all of the crêpes and filling have been used, making sure you finish with a crêpe.

Slice into wedges and serve.

SALATA

Salads

Macedonian Mixed Salad 53
Makedonska Salata

Summer Salad 54
Letna Salata

Beet Salad 57
Salata So Tsveklo

Potato Salad 58
Kompirova Salata

Roasted Sweet Pepper Salad 61
Salata So Pecheni Piperki

Cucumber Salad 63
Salata So Krastavitsi

Roasted Eggplant Salad 64
Patlidjan Salata

Wheat Berry Salad 67
Salata So Pchenica

Watermelon Salad 68
Salata So Lubenitsa

Carrot Salad 71
Morkova Salata

Cabbage Salad 72
Zelkova Salata

White Bean Salad 75
Salata So Bel Grav

SALATA
Salads

Macedonia is on about the same latitude as the Tuscan region of Italy, and it is a country rich in agriculture. There are many different Macedonian salads for every season, and all are simple and easy to make. In the sunny summer months, peppers, tomatoes, and cucumbers are commonly used in salads. The winters are cool and crisp, so heartier ingredients like beets, potatoes, carrots, and beans are favored. You will notice that all of these salads are dressed very simply, just enhancing the flavor and beauty of the ingredients.

MAKEDONSKA SALATA

MACEDONIAN MIXED SALAD

This simple garden salad is bright and fresh, and a vibrant addition to any meal. My family makes it often. I love the crunch you get from the celery and radishes, paired with the softer texture of the lettuce and tomatoes.

1 small seedless cucumber

1 large or 2 small heads of lettuce (Boston or loose leaf), chopped into bite-size pieces

2 medium tomatoes, sliced into wedges

1 medium celery stalk, thinly sliced on the diagonal

1 small carrot, grated or peeled into thin strips

2 scallions, thinly sliced

2 radishes, finely sliced

DRESSING

3 tablespoons extra-virgin olive oil

1 tablespoon red wine vinegar

½ teaspoon kosher salt

½ teaspoon freshly ground black pepper

Peel the cucumber and cut it in half lengthwise. Slice diagonally into ½-inch (1 cm) thick slices. Place in a large salad bowl and add all of the other salad ingredients.

In a small bowl, whisk together the dressing ingredients.

Just before serving, pour the dressing over the salad and gently toss to coat.

LETNA SALATA

SUMMER SALAD

This classic Macedonian salad is often known as "village salad." Simple ingredients come together in a harmony of refreshing flavor, perfect for summer meals. My favorite part is reaching the bottom of the bowl, where the creamy salty feta, velvety olive oil, and tart vinegar mix with the juices from the vegetables, making a golden liquid that is perfect for dipping (we call this mackni). So be sure to serve this salad with plenty of crusty bread. I like to peel the cucumbers in stripes for a bit of contrast and to soften the texture of the sometimes-thick skin.

4 medium tomatoes, sliced into wedges

1 English cucumber, skin peeled in stripes and sliced into ¼-inch (6 mm) rounds

½ small red onion, very thinly sliced

1 red bell pepper, cut into bite-size pieces

½ cup (75 g) shaved feta cheese

DRESSING

3 tablespoons extra-virgin olive oil

1 tablespoon red wine vinegar

1 teaspoon finely chopped fresh oregano

¼ teaspoon kosher salt

½ teaspoon freshly ground black pepper

Place the salad ingredients, aside from the feta, in a large serving bowl.

In a small bowl, whisk together the dressing ingredients.

Pour the dressing over the salad and gently toss to coat.

Chill in the refrigerator for about 10 minutes before serving.

Top with shaved feta cheese.

SALATA SO TSVEKLO

BEET SALAD

Beets grow really well in Macedonia but are really only used for salads, rather than in hot meals. My aunt Mary served this salad almost every day when I visited her in Australia. Her garden was full of beets, and I always think of her when I make this salad. She sometimes used mint or cilantro in place of the parsley and either works well.

4 medium beets, scrubbed

½ medium red onion, finely sliced

2 tablespoons chopped fresh parsley

DRESSING

1 tablespoon extra-virgin olive oil

1 teaspoon red wine vinegar

1 teaspoon freshly squeezed lemon juice

¼ teaspoon kosher salt

¼ teaspoon freshly ground black pepper

Trim the tops and bottoms off the beets, leaving the skins on.

Prepare a stovetop steamer with boiling water and steam the beets for about 30 minutes, or until tender and cooked through. Remove from the heat and allow to cool for 10 minutes.

Peel off the skins. Slice the beets in half lengthwise and then cut them into ½-inch (1 cm) wedges. Transfer to a large bowl and add the onion and parsley.

In a small bowl, whisk together the dressing ingredients.

Pour the dressing over the beets and gently toss to coat.

Transfer to a serving dish. Serve warm or cold.

KOMPIROVA
POTATO SALAD
SALATA

This hearty salad is traditionally served at weddings in Macedonia (probably because it goes well with rakija, the popular anise-flavored liqueur). Growing up, it was a staple at family picnics because it traveled so well and could stay unrefrigerated for a few hours. It is a great way to use potatoes outside of the traditional stews and soups. I've used red potatoes here because I love how silky they are. They have a tougher skin that helps to hold their shape but you could really use any potato variety you like.

4½ lb (2 kg) medium red
potatoes (about 12), cut
into equal-size chunks
1 tablespoon kosher salt

In a large pot, cover the potatoes with water and 1 tablespoon of salt, and bring to a boil. Reduce the heat to medium and simmer for about 10 minutes, or until the potatoes are tender but not falling apart. Drain in a colander and transfer to a large bowl.

DRESSING
3 scallions, finely sliced
2 tablespoons finely chopped
fresh dill
Juice of 1 lemon
¼ cup (60 ml) extra-virgin
olive oil
1 teaspoon kosher salt
1 tablespoon lemon zest

In a small bowl, whisk together the dressing ingredients.

Pour the dressing over the potatoes and gently toss to coat.

Transfer to a serving dish. Serve warm or cold.

SALATA SO
PECHENI
ROASTED SWEET PEPPER SALAD
PIPERKI

Roasted sweet peppers are used in many Macedonian dishes. Sweet bell peppers are best for this salad because of their thicker texture. My parents often made this salad to use up slightly overripe peppers in an effort not to waste them.

2 red bell peppers
2 yellow bell peppers
2 orange bell peppers
Fresh parsley leaves,
  for garnish

DRESSING

1 garlic clove, minced
1 tablespoon extra-virgin
  olive oil
1 tablespoon freshly
  squeezed lemon juice
¼ teaspoon kosher salt
¼ teaspoon freshly ground
  black pepper

Roast the peppers over a charcoal grill or a gas flame until the skins are completely charred and blistered. Alternatively broil them in the oven (directly on the rack, or on a baking sheet lined with parchment paper), rotating them every 15 minutes until charred, 30 to 45 minutes.

Place peppers in a paper bag or heatproof container. Seal and set aside for 20 minutes until cool.

Peel off the skins, keeping the stems and seeds intact. Set a colander over the sink and drain the peppers for 20 minutes. Coarsely chop the peppers and place them in a large bowl.

In a small bowl, whisk together dressing ingredients.

Pour the dressing over the peppers and gently toss to coat. Arrange on a serving dish and garnish with parsley.

SALATA SO
KRASTAVITSI

CUCUMBER SALAD

I love using a combination of cucumber varieties to give this salad a bit of dimension and texture. You can really use any kind you like, but if you're using anything other than English or Persian cucumbers, I would recommend removing the seeds before slicing, since these can be quite bitter.

1 English cucumber, skin peeled in stripes, sliced into ¼-inch (6 mm) rounds

6 Persian cucumbers, skin peeled in stripes, sliced into ¼-inch (6 mm) rounds

½ small red onion, finely sliced

¼ cup (6 g) fresh mint, finely chopped

½ cup (75 g) grated feta cheese

DRESSING

1 tablespoon extra-virgin olive oil

½ tablespoon red wine vinegar

¼ teaspoon kosher salt

In a large bowl, combine the cucumbers, onion, and mint.

In a small bowl, whisk together the dressing ingredients.

Pour the dressing over the salad and gently toss just to coat.

Transfer to a serving dish and top with grated feta cheese.

SALADS | 63

PATLIDJAN SALATA
ROASTED EGGPLANT SALAD

This is such a great salad and could very easily be a meal in itself. It can be served warm but I actually prefer it cold. I love to add the fresh mint when the ingredients are just cooked because the heat wilts the mint ever so slightly and softens its texture.

2 eggplants, peeled and chopped into 1-inch (2.5 cm) cubes

4 tablespoons extra-virgin olive oil, divided

1 red bell pepper, diced into ½-inch (1 cm) pieces

1 green bell pepper, diced into ½-inch (1 cm) pieces

1 tomato, seeds removed, diced

1 garlic clove, finely grated or minced

Juice of ½ lemon

2 tablespoons chopped fresh mint, for garnish

Kosher salt and freshly ground black pepper

Preheat the oven to 350°F (180°C).

Place the eggplants on a baking sheet. Drizzle with 2 tablespoons of the olive oil and sprinkle with 1 teaspoon of kosher salt. Toss to coat.

Roast the eggplants for 40 minutes, turning them over halfway through, until tender and golden brown.

Meanwhile, heat 1 tablespoon of oil over medium heat and sauté the peppers until just tender, 4 to 5 minutes.

In a large heat resistant bowl, mix together the peppers, tomato, garlic, 1 tablespoon of olive oil, the lemon juice, and ½ teaspoon of salt. Add the eggplants and toss to coat.

Transfer to a serving dish and sprinkle with black pepper and fresh mint.

SALATA SO PCHENICA

WHEAT BERRY SALAD

In the region of Macedonia my family is from, wheat berries are an important part of local traditions. For funerals, unsweetened wheat berries are served to all attendees, alongside bread, cheese, and wine. For births and baptisms, wheat berries are sweetened and decorated with dried fruits and candies. Growing up, we all loved wheat berries and my mother made this recipe for us in big batches, since it keeps well for several days in the fridge. I use whole hard red wheat berries, but you can use other types, or even spelt or farro (just adjust the cooking time accordingly).

2 cups (370 g) whole wheat berries

4 medium tomatoes, halved

½ red onion, finely sliced

¼ cup (6 g) finely chopped fresh parsley

½ cup (75 g) grated feta cheese

DRESSING

¼ cup (60 ml) extra-virgin olive oil

Juice of ½ lemon

1 tablespoon red wine vinegar

½ teaspoon kosher salt

½ teaspoon freshly ground black pepper

In a medium stockpot, combine the wheat berries and 6 cups (1.4 liters) of water. Bring to a boil over high heat, then reduce the heat to medium-low and simmer, uncovered, for 2½ hours. Drain and rinse with cold water. Set aside in a colander to dry.

Preheat the oven to 300°F (150°C).

Place the tomatoes cut side up on a baking sheet and roast for 2½ to 3 hours until the flesh has shrivelled but not completely dried out. Remove and set aside to cool.

Finely chop the cooled tomatoes and place them in a large bowl. Add the cooked wheat berries, onion, and parsley.

In a small bowl, whisk together the dressing ingredients. Pour the dressing over the salad and gently toss to coat.

Transfer to a serving dish and top with the feta cheese.

SALATA SO LUBENITSA

WATERMELON SALAD

This salad is the epitome of summer. Growing up in a Macedonian household, we very rarely ate watermelon without feta cheese on the side. Sweet, juicy, salty—it is the perfect combination. Flash-pickling the onions mellows their flavor so they complement the watermelon, feta, and mint instead of competing with them.

¼ red onion, very finely sliced

Juice of ½ lemon

1 tablespoon extra-virgin olive oil

½ watermelon, chopped into bite-size cubes

1 tablespoon finely chopped fresh mint

½ cup (75 g) shaved feta cheese

In a small bowl, mix together the onion, lemon juice, and olive oil. Set aside to marinate for 10 minutes.

Place the watermelon in a large bowl and add the marinated onion. Gently toss to coat.

Transfer to a serving dish and top with the mint and feta cheese.

MORKOVA SALATA

CARROT SALAD

This was the first salad I can remember eating. My father would make it for my sister and me when we were kids, and we would get so excited when he'd let us help grate the carrots.

8–10 carrots, peeled
  and grated

¼ cup (30 g) chopped walnuts

¼ cup (40 g) raisins

DRESSING

¼ cup (60 ml) plain full-fat
  Balkan yogurt (or any plain
  full-fat yogurt)

2 tablespoons extra-virgin
  olive oil

1 teaspoon freshly squeezed
  lemon juice

½ teaspoon lemon zest

½ garlic clove, finely grated
  or minced

1 teaspoon kosher salt

Place the carrots in a large bowl.

In a small bowl, whisk together the dressing ingredients.

Pour the dressing over the carrots and gently toss to coat.

Refrigerate for at least 1 hour before serving. Garnish with the walnuts and raisins.

ZELKOVA
CABBAGE SALAD
SALATA

I love this fresh side dish. I've never been a fan of the classic American-style coleslaw; I much prefer the simplicity of this light dressing. I dress the salad about an hour before I want to serve it to soften the crispness of the cabbage. I use white cabbage in this recipe since it is more common in Macedonia, but you could easily make this salad with red, Savoy, or a combination of different cabbages.

1 white cabbage, cored,
 outer layers removed,
 finely shredded

DRESSING
¼ cup (60 ml) extra-virgin
 olive oil
2 tablespoons red wine vinegar
½ teaspoon honey
½ teaspoon paprika
1 teaspoon kosher salt
1 teaspoon freshly ground
 black pepper
3 mint sprigs, finely chopped

Place the cabbage in a large bowl.

In a small bowl, whisk together the dressing ingredients.

Pour the dressing over the cabbage and gently toss to coat.

Chill in the refrigerator for at least 1 hour before serving.

SALATA SO

WHITE BEAN SALAD

BEL GRAV

Beans grow feverishly in Macedonia. My father's village is particularly known for growing beautiful beans. Growing up, we ate beans regularly in salads, soups, and stews. This salad uses white beans, but it can really be made with any bean you like. The addition of mint might sound unusual but it is very common in Macedonian cooking, especially with beans. My parents grow mint in their garden.

2 (15 oz/425 g) cans white
 kidney beans, rinsed
 and drained
2 Roma tomatoes, seeds
 removed, diced
1 red bell pepper, diced
½ medium red onion,
 finely sliced

DRESSING

2 tablespoons extra-virgin
 olive oil
Juice of ½ lemon
1 tablespoon coarsely chopped
 fresh mint, or 1 teaspoon
 dried mint
¼ teaspoon crushed red
 pepper flakes
½ teaspoon kosher salt

Place all of the salad ingredients in a large bowl.

In a small bowl, whisk together the dressing ingredients.

Pour the dressing over the beans and gently toss to coat.

SUPA

Soups

Chilled Cucumber Soup 81
Tarator

White Kidney Bean Soup 83
Gravche Supa

Meatball & Rice Soup with Spinach 84
Kioftina Supa So Oriz I Spanak

Lentil Soup 87
Lekja Supa

Chicken & Rice Soup
with Egg & Lemon 88
Pileshko I Oriz Supa So Jatse I Limon

Veal & Okra Soup 91
Bamjova Supa So Teleshko Meso

Vegetable Soup 92
Zarzavat Supa

Pork & Rice Soup 95
Supa So Oriz I Svinsko Meso

Fish Soup 96
Ribena Chorba

Tripe Soup 98
Shkembe Chorba

Split Pea Soup 101
Grashek Chorba

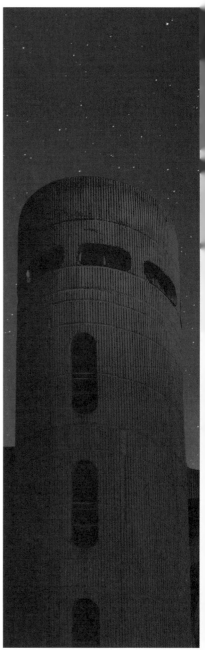

SUPA
Soups

For me, Macedonian soups are the epitome of comfort food. We grew up eating soups every week, all year round. Many are hearty, filling, and warming for the coldest days of the year; and some are light and refreshing, like Tarator, a chilled cucumber soup (page 81), which is served in the hottest months of summer. Whenever guests would arrive unexpectedly, my grandfather would jokingly say "just add a little broth to the soup and everyone will have enough." I think about him and smile every time I make soup.

SERVES 4 TO 6

TARATOR
CHILLED CUCUMBER SOUP

This cold, refreshing soup is very popular in Macedonia during the hot summer months. It is often served with fresh bread and a crisp salad on the side. The flavors are so simple and bright. I've added a bit of heavy cream to round out the tartness of the yogurt and give it a bit of richness.

2 English cucumbers, peeled, deseeded, and chopped

1 tablespoon kosher salt

1 garlic clove, finely minced

1 tablespoon finely chopped fresh dill, plus extra for garnish

1 tablespoon finely chopped fresh mint

1 teaspoon freshly squeezed lemon juice

4 cups (1 liter) plain full-fat Balkan yogurt (or any plain full-fat yogurt)

½ cup (120 ml) heavy cream

Thinly sliced cucumber, for garnish

Place the cucumbers in a colander and sprinkle with the salt. Set aside to drain for 20 minutes.

In a food processor, combine the cucumbers, garlic, dill, mint, and lemon juice. Process for 30 seconds. Scrape down the sides with spatula and process for another 30 seconds, until you have a thin purée. Transfer to a mixing bowl.

Using a spatula, stir the yogurt and heavy cream into the cucumber mixture.

Refrigerate for at least 2 hours before serving.

When ready to serve, ladle the soup into bowls and garnish with sliced cucumber and dill.

GRAVCHE SUPA

WHITE KIDNEY BEAN SOUP

This is one of my father's specialties and favorite recipes. I can always tell when a pot is on the stove from its comforting aroma, which still brings back fond memories. For periods of religious fasting when meat is prohibited, this soup is made with water instead of chicken broth—a great alternative if you're a vegetarian.

2 cups (370 g) dried white kidney or Great Northern beans, soaked for at least 6 hours in plenty of water

2 tablespoons extra-virgin olive oil

1 medium yellow onion, diced

2 carrots, peeled, sliced in half lengthwise, and diced

2 garlic cloves, minced

½ teaspoon paprika

¼ teaspoon crushed red pepper flakes

2 cups (500 g) stewed or diced tomatoes (from a jar or can)

4 cups (1 liter) low-sodium chicken stock

2 cups (480 ml) boiling water

2 Yukon gold potatoes, peeled and cut into 1-inch (2.5 cm) pieces

2 teaspoons kosher salt

2 teaspoons chopped fresh mint

Freshly ground black pepper

Drain and rinse the beans and place them in a large stockpot. Cover with about 10 cups (2.4 liters) of cold water and bring to a boil over high heat. Reduce the heat to medium-low and simmer for about 1½ hours or until the beans are tender. Drain and set aside.

In a separate large stockpot, heat the oil over medium heat. Add the onion and sauté for 3 to 4 minutes until translucent. Stir in the carrots and continue to cook for 5 or 6 minutes, until tender. Stir in the garlic, paprika, and red pepper flakes. Sauté for an additional 2 minutes.

Add the stewed tomatoes, chicken stock, boiling water, potatoes, and salt. Bring to a boil, and then reduce the heat to medium-low. Stir in the beans and simmer for 30 minutes.

Remove the soup from the heat and stir in the mint and plenty of black pepper.

KIOFTINA SUPA SO
MEATBALL & RICE SOUP WITH SPINACH
ORIZ I SPANAK

This creamy, tart soup is my favorite. It is one of the first dishes I request when I visit my parents, especially in the winter months. I make it often, but it just seems to taste better when my mother makes it. Traditionally, the meatballs are dropped into the broth raw, but I found that roasting them first gives a richer flavor. You can make the meatballs a day ahead.

MEATBALLS

Extra-virgin olive oil, for greasing
1 lb (450 g) lean ground beef
1 egg
¾ cup (140 g) long-grain white
   rice, rinsed and drained
1 small yellow onion, grated
1 tablespoon chopped parsley
1 tablespoon chopped mint
1 teaspoon kosher salt
½ teaspoon ground black pepper

SOUP

4 cups (1 liter) low-sodium
   chicken stock
4 cups (1 liter) cold water
1 tablespoon kosher salt
2 eggs
Juice of 1 lemon
2 packed cups (60 g) chopped
   fresh baby spinach

Place a rack in the middle of your oven and turn on the broiler. Lightly grease a baking sheet with olive oil.

In a medium bowl, combine the beef, egg, rice, onion, parsley, mint, salt, and pepper. Gently mix until evenly incorporated, but be careful not to overwork the meat. Roll the mixture into balls about 1 inch (2.5 cm) in diameter and place them on the baking sheet. Broil the meatballs on the middle rack of your oven until just lightly browned, 10 to 12 minutes.

Meanwhile, in a large pot, combine the chicken stock, water, and salt. Bring to a simmer over medium heat. Carefully drop the meatballs into the hot stock. Simmer, uncovered, for 25 minutes, skimming off any scum or fat that forms on the surface.

Meanwhile, in a large heat resistant bowl, whisk together the eggs and lemon juice. Whisking constantly, gradually ladle in about 4 cups (1 liter) of the hot stock from the pot, a little at a time, to temper the eggs.

Remove the soup from the heat. Slowly pour the egg mixture back into the pot and stir in the spinach before serving.

LEKJA SUPA

LENTIL SOUP

This is a warming everyday soup. The addition of tart vinegar at the end adds a bright contrast to the rich and hearty lentils. A splash of vinegar or lemon juice is a common final touch in Macedonian soups. I add a splash more vinegar to my own bowl, and extra chili flakes for a bit more punch.

1½ cups (300 g) green lentils

2 tablespoons extra-virgin olive oil

1 medium yellow onion, finely diced

2 carrots, peeled and diced

2 celery stalks, finely diced

4 garlic cloves, minced

¼ teaspoon crushed red pepper flakes

1 teaspoon dried oregano

2 cups (500 g) stewed or diced tomatoes (from a jar or can)

4 cups (1 liter) low-sodium chicken or vegetable stock

2 cups (480 ml) boiling water

1 tablespoon kosher salt

1 tablespoon red wine vinegar

Soak the lentils in about 3 cups (700 ml) of cold water for 20 minutes. Drain and rinse.

In a large stockpot, heat the olive oil over medium heat. Add the onion and sauté for 3 or 4 minutes until translucent. Add the carrots and celery and sauté until the vegetables are tender, 5 or 6 more minutes. Stir in the garlic, red pepper flakes, and dried oregano, and continue to cook for an additional 2 minutes.

Pour in the stewed tomatoes, chicken stock, boiling water, and salt. Bring to a simmer and stir in the lentils. Simmer, skimming off any scum that forms on the surface, until the lentils are tender but still hold their shape, 35 to 45 minutes.

Remove from the heat and stir in the vinegar before serving.

PILESHKO I ORIZ SUPA SO
CHICKEN & RICE SOUP WITH EGG & LEMON
JATSE I LIMON

This warming soup has a creamy lemon broth that is delicious and comforting. The egg thickens the soup without feeling heavy or overly rich. I love it with a dollop of Ajvar (page 27) on top, if you happen to have some.

MACEDONIA

88

1 tablespoon extra-virgin olive oil

1 medium yellow onion, finely diced

2 carrots, peeled, diced

2 celery stalks, diced

4–5 lb (2–2.25 kg) whole chicken, loose fat trimmed around the cavity

1 tablespoon kosher salt

3 thyme sprigs

3 parsley sprigs, plus extra, chopped, for garnish

2 garlic cloves

1 teaspoon fresh peppercorns

½ cup (90 g) long-grain white rice, rinsed and drained

2 eggs

Juice of 1 lemon

In a large pot, heat the oil over medium heat. Sauté the onion until translucent, 4 minutes. Add the carrots and celery and sauté until tender, 5 minutes.

Place the whole chicken on top of the vegetables in the pot. Pour in 8 cups (2 liters) of water and the salt. Using a piece of cheesecloth and kitchen twine, tie the thyme, parsley, garlic, and peppercorns into a sealed parcel. Add this to the pot. Bring to a boil, then reduce the heat to medium-low and simmer, uncovered, for 45 minutes, skimming off any scum or fat that forms on the surface. Then remove and discard the herb parcel.

Transfer the chicken to a large clean cutting board and set aside until cool enough to handle. Add the rice to the pot and continue to simmer, uncovered, for 20 minutes, until tender. Meanwhile, carefully remove the chicken meat, discarding the bones and fat. Shred or chop the chicken into bite-size pieces. When the rice is fully cooked, remove the pot from the heat and return the chicken to the soup.

In a large heat resistant bowl, whisk together the eggs and lemon juice. Whisking constantly, gradually ladle in about 4 cups (1 liter) of the hot stock, a little at a time, to temper the eggs.

Slowly pour the egg mixture back into the soup and stir just to incorporate. Garnish with parsley and serve hot.

BAMJOVA SUPA SO TELESHKO MESO
VEAL & OKRA SOUP

My family made this soup when okra was in season in mid- to late summer. My mother loves okra so we had this soup often. Frying the okra before adding it to the soup sears off a bit of the "slime" that occurs naturally, making for a much nicer texture. This is my favorite way to cook with okra because you are just left with its delicate earthy flavor. If you can't find veal, you can easily substitute pork tenderloin.

2 tablespoons (30 g) butter

1 lb (450 g) veal tenderloin, cut into ½-inch (1 cm) cubes

1 lb (450 g) okra, sliced diagonally into ¼-inch (6 mm) pieces

1 medium yellow onion, finely diced

2 garlic cloves, minced

1 red bell pepper, deseeded and finely diced

1 carrot, peeled and diced

1 tablespoon tomato paste

1 tablespoon kosher salt

¼ teaspoon crushed red pepper flakes

8 cups (2 liters) boiling water

1 tablespoon coarsely chopped fresh parsley, for garnish

Lemon slices, for garnish

In a large stockpot, melt 1 tablespoon of the butter over high heat and sear the veal on all sides, working in batches if necessary. Once the veal is browned, remove the meat from the pot and set it aside.

Reduce the heat to medium and add the remaining 1 tablespoon of butter. Add the okra to the pot and sear on all sides until the "slime" has dissolved, 3 to 4 minutes.

Add the onion, garlic, bell pepper, and carrot and sauté until the vegetables are tender, 5 to 6 minutes.

Stir in the tomato paste, salt, and red pepper flakes. Then pour in the boiling water and return the veal to the pot. Simmer for 45 minutes, until the meat is tender.

Garnish with parsley and lemon slices before serving.

ZARZAVAT SUPA
VEGETABLE SOUP

Fresh vegetables are a big deal in Macedonia and in the home gardens of the Macedonian families. This everyday soup is a great way to use whatever vegetables you have on hand, since the quantities can easily be adjusted. It is often made during Lent, when many abstain from eating meat.

1 tablespoon extra-virgin olive oil

1 medium yellow onion, diced

2 carrots, peeled and diced

1 garlic clove, minced

½ teaspoon paprika

2 cups (500 g) stewed or diced tomatoes (from a jar or can)

3 medium Yukon gold potatoes, peeled and diced

¼ white cabbage, cut into 1-inch (2.5 cm) cubes

1 tablespoon kosher salt

2 packed cups (60 g) coarsely chopped greens, such as beet greens or spinach

1 teaspoon red wine vinegar

2 tablespoons coarsely chopped fresh parsley, for garnish

Freshly ground black pepper

In large stockpot, heat the oil over high heat. Add the onion and sauté until translucent, 3 to 4 minutes. Add the carrots and sauté until tender, 5 to 6 minutes. Stir in the garlic and paprika and cook for an additional 2 minutes.

Pour in the stewed tomatoes and 6 cups (1.4 liters) of water. Add the potatoes, cabbage, and salt. Bring to a boil, then reduce the heat to medium and simmer until the vegetables are tender, 20 minutes.

Add the chopped greens and simmer for an additional 5 minutes. Stir in the vinegar and remove from the heat.

Garnish with chopped parsley and black pepper before serving.

SUPA SO ORIZ
I SVINSKO
MESO

PORK & RICE SOUP

My grandparents made this soup for my sister and I whenever they looked after us as children. We were lucky to have them live a few blocks away. I have vivid memories of coming indoors after playing outside on crisp fall afternoons and finding steaming bowls of this soup ready for us.

1 lb (450 g) pork tenderloin, cut into ½-inch (1 cm) cubes

3 tablespoons (45 g) unsalted butter

1 medium yellow onion, diced

1 carrot, peeled and diced

1 green bell pepper, deseeded and diced

½ teaspoon paprika

1 teaspoon dried oregano

½ teaspoon freshly ground black pepper

1 cup (250 g) stewed or diced tomatoes (from a jar or can)

4 cups (1 liter) low-sodium chicken stock

3 cups boiling water

½ cup (90 g) long-grain white rice, rinsed and drained

Kosher salt

Sprinkle the pork with 1 teaspoon of kosher salt.

In a large stockpot, melt the butter over high heat and sear the meat for 5 minutes on each side, or until brown. You may need to work in batches to avoid crowding. Remove the meat from the pot and set aside.

Add the onion to the pot and sauté for 3 to 4 minutes until translucent. Add the carrot and bell pepper, and sauté until tender, 5 to 6 minutes. Stir in the paprika, oregano, 1 tablespoon of salt, and the black pepper.

Add the stewed tomatoes, chicken stock, boiling water, and rice. Bring to a boil, then reduce the heat to medium. Return the meat to the pot and simmer for 20 minutes, or until the rice and meat are fully cooked.

RIBENA
FISH SOUP
CHORBA

In Macedonia, especially in the city of Ohrid, fish soup is a celebrated dish, served for several religious holidays. It is also a common remedy for the aftereffects of a big night out. When my mother and aunts made this soup, they typically used snapper, but you can use any firm variety of fish you like.

1 tablespoon extra-virgin olive oil, plus extra for drizzling

1 medium yellow onion, thinly sliced

2 carrots, peeled and diced

1 garlic clove, minced

½ teaspoon crushed red pepper flakes

1 tablespoon tomato paste

1 cup (250 g) stewed or diced tomatoes (from a jar or can)

4 medium Yukon gold potatoes, cut into ¼-inch (6 mm) semicircles

1 tablespoon kosher salt

2 lb (900 g) boneless firm white fish fillets, such as halibut, bass, or snapper, sliced into 2-inch (5 cm) chunks

1 tablespoon coarsely chopped fresh oregano

Juice of ½ lemon

Freshly ground black pepper

In a large stockpot, heat the olive oil over medium heat. Add the onion and gently sauté for 3 to 4 minutes until translucent. Add the carrots and sauté until tender, 5 to 6 minutes. Stir in the garlic, red pepper flakes, and tomato paste and cook for an additional 2 minutes.

Pour in the stewed tomatoes and 7 cups (1.6 liters) of water. Add the potatoes and salt. Bring to a boil, then reduce the heat to low and simmer for 15 minutes.

Carefully add the fish and oregano to the pot, and simmer until the potatoes and fish are fully cooked, 5 to 8 minutes.

Stir in the lemon juice. When ready to serve, drizzle with olive oil and top with ground black pepper.

SHKEMBE CHORBA
TRIPE SOUP

Tripe soup is popular among Macedonians, especially at Easter after midnight mass. My father loved it so my mother made it from time to time. There are many different ways people prepare tripe soup in the different regions of Macedonia but my family makes a lemon and egg broth with fresh dill to balance the richness of the tripe.

1 lb (450 g) whole tripe

1 teaspoon extra-virgin
   olive oil

1 large leek (white and light
   green part only), halved
   lengthwise and sliced

½ cup (90 g) long-grain white
   rice, rinsed and drained

2 eggs

Juice of 1 lemon

Freshly chopped dill,
   for garnish

Lemon wedges, for serving

Kosher salt and freshly ground
   black pepper

Rinse the tripe under cool running water.

In a large stockpot, cover the tripe with about 8 cups (2 liters) of water and 1 tablespoon of salt. Bring to a boil, then reduce the heat to low. Cover the pot and simmer for 2 hours, until the tripe is very tender.

Drain the tripe and set aside until cool enough to handle, then cut it into ¼-inch (6 mm) cubes.

Wipe the stockpot dry, and return it to the stovetop. Heat the oil over medium heat and sauté the leek until tender, 3 to 4 minutes. Add the tripe and rice and stir for 1 minute to toast the rice.

Pour in 8 cups (2 liters) of water and 1 tablespoon kosher salt. Bring to a boil, then reduce the heat to low and simmer, uncovered, until the rice is cooked, about 20 minutes. Remove from the heat.

In a large heat resistant bowl, whisk together the eggs and lemon juice. Whisking constantly, gradually ladle in about 4 cups (1 liter) of the hot stock, a little at a time, to temper the eggs. Slowly pour the egg mixture back into the pot and stir to incorporate.

Garnish with the dill and black pepper and serve with lemon wedges.

GRASHEK CHORBA
SPLIT PEA SOUP

This soup is so simple and satisfying. It was one of my father's few go-to recipes. Cinnamon may seem like an unusual addition, but in Macedonian cooking, it is used in both sweet and savory dishes.

2 cups (400 g) dried yellow split peas

2 teaspoons extra-virgin olive oil, plus extra for drizzling

1 medium yellow onion, finely diced

1 teaspoon paprika

2 teaspoons kosher salt

4 cups (1 liter) low-sodium chicken stock

Cinnamon, for garnish

Rinse the split peas and discard any that are discolored.

In a large stockpot, heat the olive oil over medium-high heat. Add the onion and sauté until tender, 3 to 4 minutes. Reduce the heat to medium. Add the split peas, paprika, and salt, and stir to coat.

Pour in the chicken stock and 4 cups (1 liter) of water. Cover and simmer gently for 1½ to 2 hours until the peas are soft.

Remove from the heat and let cool. When ready to serve, return the soup to the pot and heat through. Garnish with a drizzle of olive oil and a light sprinkle of cinnamon.

MESO

Meats

Cabbage Stew **106**
Zelkova Mangia

Lamb, Leek & Potato Stew **109**
Jagneshka Mangia So Praz I Kompiri

Grilled Pork Chops **110**
Kremenadli

Stuffed Peppers **112**
Polneti Piperki

Pork Rib & Lima Bean Stew **114**
Svinski Rebra So Gravche

Lamb, Eggplant & Potato Casserole **116**
Musaka So Meso, Kompiri I Patlijani

Cabbage Rolls **118**
Sarmi Od Zelka

Beef & Onion Stew **121**
Govedsko Meso So Kromit

Meat Stew with Vegetables **122**
Turli Tava So Meso

Roasted Leg of Lamb **124**
Pechena Noga Od Jagne

Roasted Pork with Sauerkraut & Rice **126**
Svinsko Pecheno So Kisela Zelka I Oriz

Meat Pie **128**
Pastrmajlija

MESO
Meats

When my parents were growing up in Macedonia, meat was
a luxury reserved only for celebrations and special occasions.
Day-to-day meals in the villages were made up of an array of
vegetables, beans, and legumes. Even for my father's family, who
were shepherds, lamb was only served a few times a year, for
Easter, name days, or weddings. The costly meat would be reserved
to sell, and the family often couldn't afford the indulgence.

Pork was also customary during celebrations throughout the
year, especially at weddings, where a whole roast suckling pig
played a symbolic role in the celebration, during the bieshetoe
horo (pig dance, see page 16). Beef was a rarer luxury; the region
my parents come from is mountainous, without the rolling fields
needed to raise cattle.

When an animal was slaughtered, every part would be
utilized. Stews and braises use low and slow cooking techniques
in order to break down tougher cuts of meat, and more tender
cuts are typically grilled or pan-fried. Any unused meat was
submerged in lard and stored in clay pots to preserve it for the
colder months.

Today, meat has become much more common in day-to-
day meals because of the convenience of grocery stores and
refrigeration. However, respect for the animal is ingrained in the
culture, and meat is almost always served with some fanfare as
the centerpiece of the meal.

ZELKOVA
CABBAGE STEW
MANGIA

This is a classic, hearty Macedonian stew. White cabbage grows abundantly in Macedonia and is very popular in Macedonian cooking. This is one of my father's go-to recipes and we love his slightly spicy broth. My family makes this stew all year round but it is especially good in the winter. I like to crumble a bit of feta cheese over the top—the feta almost melts into the broth.

2 lb (900 g) boneless pork shoulder, fat trimmed, cut into 1-inch (2.5 cm) cubes

1 tablespoon extra-virgin olive oil

1 medium yellow onion, diced

½ hot banana pepper, deseeded and finely diced, or ½ teaspoon crushed red pepper flakes

2 garlic cloves, minced

1 teaspoon freshly ground black pepper

1 teaspoon paprika

1 cup (240 ml) red wine

1 cup (250 g) stewed or diced tomatoes (from a jar or can)

4 cups (1 liter) boiling water

1 medium white cabbage, cored, chopped into ½-inch (1 cm) pieces

Crumbled feta cheese, for serving (optional)

Kosher salt

Pat the pork dry using paper towels and sprinkle the meat with 1 teaspoon of kosher salt.

In a large stockpot, heat the oil over high heat and sear the pork for 3 or 4 minutes per side until golden brown (you may need to work in batches to avoid crowding the pot). Remove and set aside.

Drain all but about 1 teaspoon of fat from the pot. Reduce the heat to medium. Add the onion and banana pepper or red pepper flakes and sauté for 3 to 4 minutes until tender. Stir in the garlic, 1 tablespoon kosher salt, the black pepper, and paprika. Sauté for an additional 2 minutes.

Pour in the red wine and simmer for 4 to 5 minutes to reduce the liquid by half. Pour in the stewed tomatoes and boiling water. Return the pork to the pot. Reduce the heat to low and simmer, covered, for 2 hours.

Remove the lid and add the cabbage. Stir just to submerge the cabbage in the liquid and simmer, uncovered, for an additional 40 minutes, until the pork is tender.

Serve with crumbled feta, if desired.

JAGNESHKA
MANGIA SO
PRAZI KOMPIRI

LAMB, LEEK & POTATO STEW

My grandfather was a self-taught chef and had a thriving restaurant in Toronto. He would make this stew for us whenever we visited for Sunday lunch. In the villages where my grandparents grew up, this stew would typically be made in the spring, in the months after Easter while lamb was readily available. I love making this for a small group of friends or family coming over because it can be made in advance and reheated without compromising the flavor of the stew.

1 lb (450 g) boneless leg of lamb, fat trimmed, cut into 1-inch (2.5 cm) cubes

2 tablespoons extra-virgin olive oil

4 leeks, cut into ½-inch (1 cm) rings (white and light green parts only)

½ hot banana pepper, finely diced, or ½ teaspoon crushed red pepper flakes

2 garlic cloves, thinly sliced

1 tablespoon all-purpose flour

3 cups (700 ml) boiling water

2 tablespoons tomato paste

4–6 large Yukon gold potatoes, sliced into wedges

1 teaspoon ground black pepper

1 tablespoon coarsely chopped fresh mint, for serving

Kosher salt

Preheat the oven to 350°F (180°C). Sprinkle the lamb with 1 teaspoon of kosher salt.

In a Dutch oven or large sauté pan, heat the oil over high heat and sear the lamb for 3 to 4 minutes per side, until golden brown (you may need to work in batches to avoid crowding the pot). Remove and set aside.

Reduce the heat to medium. Add the leeks and hot pepper or red pepper flakes and sauté for 3 to 4 minutes until tender. Stir in the garlic and flour. Sauté for an additional 2 minutes.

Pour in the boiling water. Add the tomato paste, potatoes, lamb, and 1 tablespoon of kosher salt. If using a sauté pan, carefully transfer the ingredients to a baking dish.

Cover with a lid or aluminum foil and bake in the oven for 1 hour. Uncover and bake for an additional 15 minutes.

Just before serving, garnish with black pepper and fresh mint.

KREMENADLI
GRILLED PORK CHOPS

These mildly spiced pork chops pair well with nearly any salad or side dish in this book. Using a mortar and pestle to create the paste really brings the flavors together, and is worth the extra effort.

2 garlic cloves, coarsely chopped

3 tablespoons extra-virgin olive oil

1 teaspoon paprika

1 tablespoon kosher salt

2 teaspoons freshly ground black pepper

4 thick-cut, bone-in pork chops (about 3 lb/1.4 kg in total)

Using a mortar and pestle, mash the garlic with the oil, paprika, salt, and black pepper to form a paste.

Pat the pork chops dry using paper towels. Smear the paste all over the meat. Transfer to a dish and cover with a lid or plastic wrap. Refrigerate for at least 1 hour to marinate.

Preheat a grill or a cast iron skillet to high heat. Sear the pork chops for 4 to 6 minutes on each side until golden brown and just cooked through.

Remove the pork chops from the heat and let them rest for 5 minutes before serving.

POLNETI
STUFFED PEPPERS
PIPERKI

This is such a popular dish in Macedonian cooking. Everyone has a different take, but traditionally the stuffing is made with ground beef and rice. Depending on what looks best at the butcher, I sometimes substitute other ground meats as well, particularly pork. My aunt Sophie used to make the best stuffed peppers in our family and her tip was to put tomato slices on top to keep the rice moist while baking.

8 large bell peppers, ¼ inch
(6 mm) cut off the tops,
seeds removed

Olive oil

1 lb (450 g) lean ground beef

2 medium yellow onions, grated

1 cup (180 g) long-grain white
rice, rinsed and drained

4 garlic cloves, minced

1½ teaspoons kosher salt

1 teaspoon freshly ground
black pepper

1 tablespoon dried oregano

1 teaspoon paprika

2 teaspoons tomato paste

1 cup red wine

½ cup (12 g) finely chopped
fresh parsley

Boiling water

2 large tomatoes, cut into
8 thick slices

Preheat the oven to 350°F (180°C). In a deep baking dish or Dutch oven, arrange the peppers upright so that they fit snugly and won't topple over.

In a large sauté pan, heat 1 teaspoon of olive oil over high heat. Add the ground beef and cook, stirring constantly, until the meat is just cooked. Drain the fat from the meat and set the meat aside.

In the same pan, heat 2 tablespoons of olive oil over medium heat. Add the onions, rice, garlic, salt, black pepper, oregano, paprika, and tomato paste. Sauté, stirring, for 1 minute, just to toast the rice. Pour in the wine and bring to a simmer. Remove the pan from the heat and stir in the meat, parsley, and 1 cup (240 ml) of the boiling water.

Loosely fill each pepper with the meat and rice mixture to just below the brim of the pepper. Gently press one slice of tomato on top of the opening of each pepper.

Pour ½ cup (120 ml) of the boiling water into the bottom of the baking dish. Tightly cover the dish with a lid or aluminum foil and bake for 30 minutes.

Remove the lid or foil and bake for an additional 30 minutes, until the peppers are tender and the rice is cooked.

SVINSKI REBRA SO GRAVCHE

PORK RIB & LIMA BEAN STEW

This was one of my grandfather's specialties, and no one could make it quite as well as he could. The memory of him and my nostalgia for this dish is why it is one of my favorite recipes.

3 cups (550 g) large dried white lima beans, soaked for at least 6 hours in plenty of water, drained

¼ cup (60 ml) olive oil

2 lb (900 g) pork spareribs, sliced between the bones

2 medium yellow onions, diced

2 carrots, peeled and diced

2 celery stalks, diced

2 tablespoons tomato paste

2 garlic cloves, sliced

¼ teaspoon crushed red pepper flakes

1 teaspoon dried oregano

8 cups (2 liters) boiling water

1 tablespoon coarsely chopped fresh mint, for garnish

Kosher salt

Place the beans in a large pot and cover with cold water. Bring to a boil, then reduce the heat to low and simmer for 1 hour. Drain and set aside.

Preheat the oven to 350°F (180°C). In a large roasting pan placed over 2 burners (or in a large skillet over 1 burner), heat the olive oil over high heat. Sprinkle the ribs with 1 teaspoon of kosher salt. Sear the ribs until golden brown on all sides (you may need to do this in batches). Remove and set aside.

Reduce the heat to medium and, in the same pan, sauté the onions, carrots, and celery until tender, 8 to 10 minutes. Stir in the tomato paste, garlic, red pepper flakes, oregano, and 1 teaspoon of kosher salt. Sauté for an additional 2 minutes. If using a large skillet, transfer the vegetables to a large roasting pan or baking dish.

Gently stir the beans into the vegetables. Nestle the ribs into the mixture. Pour in just enough of the boiling water to cover the beans, and sprinkle with 1 tablespoon of kosher salt. Use a wooden spoon or spatula to push the ribs and beans down so they are submerged in the liquid. Cover the roasting pan or dish with a lid or aluminum foil and bake in the oven for 30 minutes. Remove the lid or foil and bake, uncovered, for an additional 45 minutes to 1 hour, until the beans are fully cooked and the ribs are tender.

Garnish with fresh mint before serving.

MUSAKA SO MESO, KOMPIRI I PATLIJANI

LAMB, EGGPLANT & POTATO CASSEROLE

Typically, this is a very rich dish but I've taken a slightly lighter approach with my recipe. The traditional way to make this dish is to fry the eggplant and potatoes before putting it all together, which is delicious but very heavy. I prefer to roast the eggplant slices and boil the potatoes before assembly, and everyone I've made this for loves it just as much.

3 medium eggplants, peeled and sliced into ½-inch (1 cm) thick rounds

4 tablespoons extra-virgin olive oil, divided, plus extra for greasing

4 large Yukon gold potatoes, peeled and sliced into ½-inch (1 cm) thick rounds

1 lb (450 g) lean ground lamb

1 large yellow onion, finely diced

1 green bell pepper, seeds removed, finely diced

2 garlic cloves, minced

¼ teaspoon crushed red pepper flakes

½ teaspoon freshly ground black pepper

Preheat the oven to 375°F (190°C). Grease a 12- x 15-inch (30 x 40 cm) baking dish and a large baking sheet with olive oil.

Brush both sides of the eggplant slices with 3 tablespoons of the olive oil and sprinkle with 1 teaspoon of kosher salt. Arrange the eggplant slices on the baking sheet in a single layer (in batches if necessary). Bake for 15 minutes until just slightly golden brown. Flip the eggplant slices and bake for an additional 15 minutes. Remove and set aside.

Place the potatoes in a large stockpot, fill with water to cover, and add 1 tablespoon of kosher salt. Bring to a boil, then reduce the heat to medium and simmer for 5 minutes. Drain the potatoes well and lay them out on a tray lined with paper towels to dry as much as possible.

In a large sauté pan, heat the remaining 1 tablespoon of olive oil over high heat. Add the lamb and cook, stirring constantly, until the meat is just cooked through. Remove the lamb and set aside. Drain all but about 1 tablespoon of fat from the pan.

Continued

½ cup (120 ml) red wine

2 medium tomatoes, peeled and diced

½ cup (125 g) stewed or diced tomatoes (from a jar or can)

1½ cup (150 g) grated Parmesan cheese, divided

Kosher salt

SAUCE

8 tablespoons (113 g) unsalted butter

½ cup (60 g) all-purpose flour

4 cups (1 liter) whole milk, warmed

½ teaspoon nutmeg

1 teaspoon kosher salt

3 egg yolks

Reduce the heat to medium. In the same pan, sauté the onion and green pepper for 3 to 4 minutes until tender. Stir in the garlic, red pepper flakes, 1 teaspoon of kosher salt, and the black pepper. Sauté for an additional 2 minutes.

Pour in the red wine and bring to a simmer. Stir in the diced tomatoes, stewed tomatoes, and lamb. Remove from the heat and set aside.

Arrange the sliced potatoes on the bottom of the greased baking dish, overlapping them slightly. Spoon half of the lamb mixture on top and spread evenly over the potatoes. Now layer the eggplant slices on top of the meat, overlapping them slightly. Spread the remaining meat mixture over the eggplants, and sprinkle with ½ cup (50 g) of the Parmesan cheese. Set aside.

To make the sauce, melt the butter in a medium stockpot and whisk in the flour. Continue to whisk for 2 minutes until a roux (paste) forms. Whisk in the milk and continue to whisk for about 5 minutes until the sauce is free of lumps and begins to thicken. Mix in the nutmeg and salt and remove from the heat.

In a medium heatproof bowl, whisk the egg yolks. Whisking continuously, slowly ladle about 1 cup of the hot sauce into the egg yolks to temper them. Pour the egg mixture into the sauce and stir to incorporate. Ladle the sauce on top of the casserole.

Sprinkle the dish with the remaining 1 cup (100 g) of Parmesan cheese and bake, uncovered, for 45 to 55 minutes, or until golden brown.

SARMI OD ZELKA

CABBAGE ROLLS

This classic Macedonian dish is made often and is an important part of the traditional Christmas Eve meal, when immediate family enjoy a "lean meal" as part of the religious tradition. On Christmas Eve, Sarmi are traditionally served along with Tavche Gravche *(Traditional White Bean Stew, page 177),* Pitulitsi *(Fritters, page 238), boiled potatoes, and fruit.*

1 whole green cabbage,
    stem and core removed
4 strips of smoked bacon, diced
½ lb (225 g) lean ground pork
½ medium yellow onion,
    finely diced
1 celery stalk, finely diced
1½ tablespoons tomato paste
1 teaspoon dried oregano
½ cup (90 g) long-grain white
    rice, rinsed and drained
½ cup (120 ml) boiling water
1 teaspoon red wine vinegar
1 egg, whisked
Olive oil, for greasing
1 cup (240 ml) tomato sauce
Kosher salt

Fill a large stockpot with water and add 1 tablespoon of kosher salt. Submerge the whole cabbage in the water. Bring to a boil, then reduce the heat and simmer until the leaves are tender, 20 to 30 minutes. Drain the cabbage and set aside until just cool enough to handle. Carefully peel away one leaf at a time being careful not to tear them. Place leaves flat on a towel to dry. They must be opaque and pliable.

To make the filling, heat a large sauté pan over medium-high heat and cook the bacon until slightly crispy, about 5 minutes. Remove and set aside.

In the same pan, cook the ground pork, stirring constantly, until the meat is just cooked through. Drain the fat and set the meat aside.

Add the onion and celery and sauté for 3 to 4 minutes until tender. Return the bacon and ground pork to the pan and add the tomato paste, oregano, and 1½ teaspoons of kosher salt. Add the rice and sauté for 1 minute until just toasted. Pour in the boiling water and vinegar and remove from the heat. Let the mixture cool for 10 minutes, and then stir in the egg.

Preheat the oven to 350°F (180°C). Grease a 9- by 13-inch (23 by 33 cm) baking dish with olive oil. Using a paring knife, slice off the raised part

of the large vein at the base of one cabbage leaf so that it is flush with the rest of the leaf. Lay the leaf flat and place a heaping spoonful of the filling just above the base. Carefully roll the base over the filling and tuck in the sides of the leaf. Continue to roll up until you have a tight parcel. Repeat with the rest of the leaves and filling, carefully placing the cabbage rolls in the baking dish, seam side down, so that they fit snugly in a single layer. Pour the tomato sauce over the rolls.

Cover the baking dish with a lid or aluminum foil and bake for 45 minutes. Remove the lid and bake, uncovered, for an additional 15 minutes. Check to make sure the rice is cooked through before serving.

GOVEDSKO MESO SO KROMIT

BEEF & ONION STEW

This recipe is really simple to put together, but make sure you allow enough time for the stew to braise. Slow braising is the secret to really tender beef. This recipe is great in spring when green onions are in season, but pearl onions work just fine.

2 lb (900 g) beef chuck, cut into 1-inch (2.5 cm) pieces

2 teaspoons kosher salt, divided

1 tablespoon extra-virgin olive oil

2 carrots, peeled and diced

2 garlic cloves, minced

1 tomato, diced

¼ teaspoon crushed red pepper flakes

1 teaspoon dried oregano

¼ teaspoon cinnamon

1 tablespoon flour

1 cup (240 ml) red wine

2 cups (480 ml) boiling water

½ teaspoon freshly ground black pepper

3 cups (400 g) peeled young heirloom onions, cipollini, or pearl onions (frozen ok)

Preheat the oven to 300°F (150°C).

Pat the beef dry with paper towels and sprinkle the meat with 1 teaspoon of the kosher salt.

In a Dutch oven, heat the oil over high heat. Sear the meat for 3 to 4 minutes on each side until browned. You may need to work in batches to avoid crowding the pot. If working in batches, return the meat to the pot.

Add the carrots, garlic, tomato, red pepper flakes, oregano, and cinnamon and sauté for 3 to 4 minutes until the carrots begin to soften.

Sprinkle the flour over the meat and vegetables in the pot and stir until the meat looks dry and pasty. Pour in the wine. Reduce the heat to medium and simmer until the wine reduces by half, 4 to 5 minutes.

Pour in the boiling water and add the remaining 1 teaspoon of kosher salt and the black pepper. Stir in the onions, cover with a lid or aluminum foil, and braise in the oven for 2½ hours. Remove the lid and bake, uncovered, for an additional 20 minutes.

TURLI TAVA
MEAT STEW WITH VEGETABLES
SO MESO

Combining different meats in one recipe is actually quite common in Macedonian cuisine. This is a very traditional recipe that I learned from my grandfather. It is perhaps a nod to a time when people used whatever was available. There is something really rustic and ancient about this meal that I love, since I know as it has been passed down through generations.

2 tablespoons (30 g) unsalted butter

½ lb (225 g) lean stewing beef, cut into 1-inch (2.5 cm) chunks

½ lb (225 g) pork shoulder, cut into 1-inch (2.5 cm) chunks

½ lb (225 g) stewing veal, cut into 1-inch (2.5 cm) chunks

1 medium yellow onion, grated

2 garlic cloves, minced

1 teaspoon paprika

1 teaspoon dried oregano

1 cup (240 ml) red wine

2 cups (500 g) stewed or diced tomatoes (from a jar or can)

1 cup (240 ml) boiling water

2 medium Yukon gold potatoes, peeled and diced

1 lb (450 g) fresh green beans, trimmed

4–6 oregano sprigs, for garnish

Kosher salt

Preheat the oven to 300°F (150°C).

In a large Dutch oven, melt the butter over high heat. Sprinkle all of the meats with 2 teaspoons of kosher salt and sear for 3 to 4 minutes on each side until golden brown (you may need to work in batches). Remove the meat and set aside.

Reduce the heat to medium. Add the onion to the pot and sauté for 2 minutes. Stir in the garlic, paprika, and dried oregano and sauté for an additional 2 minutes.

Pour in the wine and simmer for 4 to 5 minutes, until reduced by half. Add the stewed tomatoes, boiling water, 1 tablespoon of kosher salt, and the meat. Stir to combine and bring to a simmer.

Cover with a lid or aluminum foil and bake for 2½ hours. Remove the lid and stir in the potatoes and green beans. Bake, uncovered, for an additional 1 hour, or until the potatoes are cooked and the beans are tender.

Garnish with fresh oregano before serving.

PECHENA NOGA OD JAGNE

ROASTED LEG OF LAMB

Easter is one of the most important celebrations in Macedonia. It is common for each family to roast a whole lamb on a spit. My family did this every year and was an incredible tradition to grow up with. Spit-roasting lamb is a very involved process and actually not one that I am really skilled at. This recipe is great for smaller gatherings and an easier way to enjoy lamb. I make it for Easter but you could make it for any special occasion.

4–5 lb (2–2.25 kg) whole bone-in leg of lamb

2 teaspoons freshly ground black pepper

2 tablespoons extra-virgin olive oil

4 medium Yukon gold potatoes, peeled and cut into wedges

3 medium tomatoes, cut into wedges

3 garlic cloves, minced

2 tablespoons chopped fresh mint

1 tablespoon chopped fresh parsley

Juice of 1 lemon

Kosher salt

Preheat the oven to 300°F (150°C). Let the lamb sit at room temperature for 15 minutes. Pat dry with paper towels and, using a sharp knife, score the fat in a cross-hatch pattern. Rub the lamb with 1 tablespoon of kosher salt and the black pepper.

Heat a large Dutch oven over high heat for 3 to 4 minutes. Pour in the oil and carefully sear the lamb for 5 to 6 minutes per side until golden brown. Add about 1 cup (240 ml) of water to the pot. Cover with a lid or aluminum foil and roast in the oven for 4 hours.

In a bowl, toss together the potatoes, tomatoes, garlic, mint, parsley, and 1 teaspoon of kosher salt.

Remove the meat from the oven and scatter the potatoes and tomatoes around the base of the meat. Return to the oven and roast, uncovered, for an additional 40 to 45 minutes until the potatoes are cooked through.

Remove from the oven and pour the lemon juice over the lamb and vegetables. Let the meat rest for 10 minutes before serving.

SVINSKO
PECHENO
SO KISELA
ROASTED PORK WITH SAUERKRAUT & RICE
ZELKA I ORIZ

My grandfather made his own sauerkraut that tasted amazing, but I also love a good quality store-bought sauerkraut. This dish looks really sophisticated, but it is quite easy to make. Sometimes I make it with bone-in pork chops instead of pork tenderloin.

1 tablespoon unsalted butter

2 lb (900 g) pork tenderloin

5 strips of smoked bacon, diced

½ medium yellow onion, diced

1 teaspoon paprika

½ teaspoon freshly ground
black pepper

1 cup (180 g) long-grain white
rice, rinsed and drained

3 cups (420 g) sauerkraut,
rinsed and drained

3½ cups (830 ml) boiling water

½ teaspoon finely chopped dill

Kosher salt

Preheat the oven to 375°F (190°C). In a large Dutch oven, melt the butter over high heat. Sprinkle the pork with ½ teaspoon of kosher salt and sear for 4 to 5 minutes on each side until golden brown. Remove and set aside.

Reduce the heat to medium. Add the bacon and cook for 3 to 4 minutes, stirring occasionally, until the fat renders. Remove the bacon and set it aside. Drain all but about 1 teaspoon of the fat left in the pot. Add the onion to the pot and sauté for 3 to 4 minutes until tender. Sprinkle in the paprika, 1 teaspoon of kosher salt, and the black pepper. Stir in the rice and bacon and stir for 1 minute to toast the rice. Add the sauerkraut and boiling water, making sure that the rice is fully submerged in water.

Nestle the pork loin on top of the sauerkraut and rice. Cover with a lid or aluminum foil and bake for 20 to 25 minutes until the rice is cooked.

Remove the pork loin from the pot and set aside to rest for 5 minutes. Gently fold the dill into the rice mixture. Slice the pork diagonally, against the grain of the meat, and serve with the rice and sauerkraut.

PASTRMAJLIJA

MEAT PIE

The word pastrma *means salted dried meat. Pastrmajlija is Macedonia's much-loved version of pizza and it can be found in restaurants, markets, and cafes throughout the region. In parts of Macedonia there are festivals devoted solely to this dish. It is a popular late-night meal after a night of dancing.*

DOUGH

1½ cups (350 ml) warm water

2¼ teaspoons (7 g) active-
  dry yeast

½ teaspoon white sugar

4 cups (500 g) all-purpose
  flour, sifted, plus extra
  for dusting

1 tablespoon kosher salt

2 tablespoons extra-virgin olive
  oil, plus extra for greasing

FILLING

1 lb (450 g) pork tenderloin,
  cut into ½-inch (1 cm)
  chunks

5 tablespoons (70 g) butter,
  melted

1 tablespoon extra-virgin
  olive oil

2 teaspoons kosher salt

½ teaspoon paprika

3 eggs, whisked

Place the warm water in a small bowl. Add the yeast and sugar. Cover the bowl with a plate and let stand until the yeast begins to foam, about 10 minutes.

In a large bowl, whisk together the flour and salt. Make a well in the center. Pour the yeast mixture and the oil into the well. Using a spatula, gently fold the flour into the liquid until incorporated and a dough begins to form. Transfer the dough to a lightly floured work surface and knead until smooth and elastic, about 10 minutes. Lightly dust the surface of the dough with flour if it feels sticky. Lightly grease a large bowl with a thin layer of olive oil and place the dough inside. Brush the top of the dough with a thin layer of olive oil. Cover the bowl with a large plate and set aside in a warm place to rise for 1 hour.

Meanwhile, toss together the pork, melted butter, olive oil, salt, and paprika. Refrigerate for 1 hour to marinate.

Preheat the oven to 350°F (180°C). Grease a 21- by 15-inch (53 by 38 cm) baking sheet with olive oil.

Place the dough on a clean work surface. Roll the dough into a rectangle ¼-inch (6 mm) thick, and about 2 inches (5 cm) larger than your baking sheet. Carefully transfer the dough to the baking sheet. Fold the edges of the dough over to create a border around the perimeter of the baking sheet. Spread the meat over the dough in a single layer. Brush the edges of the dough with the whisked eggs and set the remaining eggs aside.

Bake the pie for 20 minutes. Remove from the oven and pour the remaining eggs over the meat. Return to the oven and bake for an additional 7 to 10 minutes, until the eggs are cooked and the dough is golden brown.

ZHIVINA

Poultry

Spiced Chicken 135
Zachineto Pileshko

Fried Skillet Chicken Breasts 136
Tava So Pileshki Gradi

Chicken Skewers 138
Pileshki Razhnitsi

Braised Quail 141
Pilinja Pecheni

Chicken & Orzo 142
Gershla So Pileshko Meso

Chicken Pie 145
Pileshki Musaka

Chicken & Rice 146
Pileshki Pilav

Stuffed Chicken with Leeks & Cheese 148
Pileshko Polneto So Praz I Sirenje

Roasted Cornish Hens with 150
Cabbage & Potatoes
Pechena Kokoshka So Zelka I Kompiri

Baked Chicken with Vegetables 153
Pechena Pileshko I Zelenchuk

Chicken & Mushrooms 154
Pileshko So Pechurki

ZHIVINA
Poultry

Poultry is a widely used ingredient in Macedonian cooking. In my parents' villages, chickens would roam the gardens and were a natural part of the agricultural landscape. Macedonia also has a wide selection of game birds that are sometimes used in similar recipes. Growing up, I remember traveling through the villages of Macedonia with my parents, eating at relatives' homes or in local restaurants, and the chicken dishes were among the best I've ever had. All of the recipes in this chapter are common throughout the regions of Macedonia and are simple, rustic, and full of flavor.

ZACHINETO PILESHKO

SPICED CHICKEN

This dish, traditionally roasted in a furna (a wood-fired oven), is one of the best dishes you can have in Macedonia. The chicken is typically roasted in a shallow, glazed clay baker and served with fresh bread.

3 tablespoons extra-virgin olive oil

2 teaspoons kosher salt

1 teaspoon paprika

½ teaspoon cinnamon

¼ teaspoon cayenne pepper

3–4 lb (1.5–2 kg) whole chicken, cut into serving-size pieces

2 medium yellow onions, cut into wedges

4–6 whole garlic cloves, peeled

In a large bowl, whisk together the oil, salt, paprika, cinnamon, and cayenne to make a marinade.

Place the chicken, onions, and garlic in a large bowl. Pour over the marinade and toss by hand. Make sure all of the pieces are evenly coated. Cover with plastic wrap and refrigerate for 1 hour to marinate.

Preheat the oven to 400°F (200°C).

Arrange the onions and garlic on the bottom of a 9- by 13-inch (23 by 33 cm) baking dish (or a clay baker if you have one). Place the chicken pieces (skin side up) on top of the onions. Roast, uncovered, for 30 to 35 minutes, until the chicken is fully cooked.

Switch the oven to broil for 3 to 4 minutes, watching carefully, to crisp up the chicken skin.

TAVA SO PILESHKI GRADI

FRIED SKILLET CHICKEN BREASTS

Whenever my sister and I would sleep over at my cousin's house, my aunt would make these for us. She was an incredible cook. They make great sandwiches, tucked into Poupchina (Bread Rolls, page 215) with fresh lettuce and Ajvar (Roasted Red Pepper and Eggplant Dip, page 27).

4 boneless skinless
   chicken breasts

1 cup (125 g) all-purpose flour

3 eggs, whisked

1 cup (115 g) plain dried
   breadcrumbs

2 teaspoons paprika

1 teaspoon freshly ground
   black pepper

¼ cup (60 ml) vegetable oil,
   for frying

Kosher salt

SAUCE

Juice of 1 lemon

Zest of ½ lemon

½ cup (12 g) chopped
   fresh parsley

First make the sauce. In a small bowl, whisk together the lemon juice, lemon zest, and parsley. Set aside.

One at a time, place the chicken breasts in a large zip-top plastic bag or between two pieces of plastic wrap or parchment paper. Pound out using a meat mallet until each breast is about ½-inch (1 cm) thick.

In a shallow dish, whisk the flour together with 1½ teaspoons of kosher salt. Place the eggs in a second dish. In a third shallow dish, whisk together the breadcrumbs, paprika, 1½ teaspoons of kosher salt, and the pepper.

Coat each chicken breast in the seasoned flour and shake off excess. Then coat each breast with whisked eggs and shake off excess. Finally, place each breast in the breadcrumbs, making sure each piece is evenly coated.

In a large sauté pan, heat the oil until it begins to shimmer and reaches a temperature of about 350°F (180°C). Carefully place the coated chicken breasts into the hot oil (working in batches if necessary). Fry for 3 to 4 minutes on each side, until golden brown and cooked through. Transfer the cooked chicken to a plate lined with paper towels to drain excess oil.

Place on a plate and spoon over the lemon and parsley sauce before serving.

PILESHKI
RAZHNITSI

CHICKEN SKEWERS

One of the best cooking secrets my grandfather taught me was to marinate chicken breasts in yogurt. The enzymes in the yogurt tenderize the meat. These skewers are common street food in Macedonia and we often had them at family barbecues. You will need 8 to 10 metal or pre-soaked bamboo skewers (soak bamboo skewers for 20 minutes).

2 lb (900 g) boneless skinless chicken thighs (about 4), cut into 1-inch (2.5 cm) cubes

1½ cups (350 ml) plain full-fat Balkan yogurt (or any plain full-fat yogurt)

1 teaspoon kosher salt

1 tablespoon extra-virgin olive oil

1 tablespoon chopped fresh mint, plus extra to garnish

In a large bowl, combine the chicken, yogurt, salt, olive oil, and mint. Mix to coat. Cover and refrigerate for at least 2 hours and up to 24 hours to marinate.

Skewer 2 to 3 pieces of chicken towards the top end of each skewer.

Heat a grill pan or grill to medium-high heat. Grill the chicken skewers for 4 to 5 minutes on each side until golden brown and fully cooked.

Garnish with the remaining mint before serving.

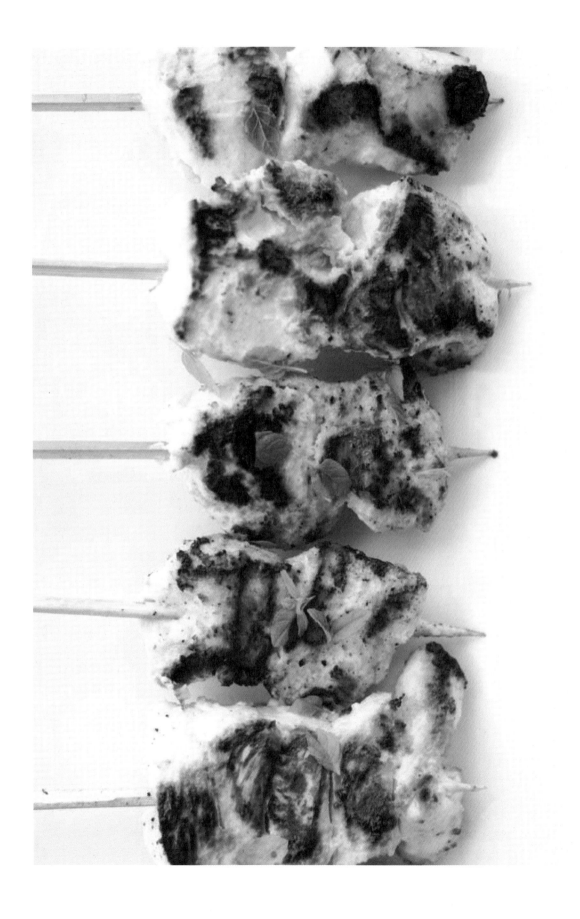

PILINJA PECHENI

BRAISED QUAIL

Game birds are quite popular in Macedonia. They can be found in the lowlands and open fields, particularly in the regions of Pelegonjia and Dolnesko. If you can't find quails in your local market, you can easily substitute Cornish hens or chicken thighs in this recipe; just adjust the cooking time accordingly. Serve this dish with Pilav Od Oriz (Rice Pilaf, page 181) or Pecheni Kompiri (Roasted Potatoes, page 178).

4 quail (2 lb/900 g in total), backbone removed, spatchcocked

2 tablespoons (30 g) butter, at room temperature

½ teaspoon kosher salt

¼ teaspoon paprika

¼ teaspoon nutmeg

1 cup (240 ml) red wine

2 cups (450 g) small peeled pearl onions (frozen are fine)

Chopped parsley, for garnish

Preheat the oven to 400°F (200°C).

In a small dish, mix together the butter, salt, paprika, and nutmeg. Smear the butter mixture all over the quail.

Heat a skillet, preferably cast iron, over high heat and brown the quail for 2 to 3 minutes on each side, just until the skin turns golden brown. Remove the quail and set aside.

Reduce the heat to medium. Pour the wine into the skillet. Add the onions and simmer until the wine has reduced by half, 4 to 5 minutes.

Return the quail to the skillet and roast in the oven until just cooked through, 10 to 12 minutes.

Sprinkle with chopped parsley and serve immediately.

GERSHLA SO PILESHKO MESO

CHICKEN & ORZO

Once you try it, this recipe is sure to become one of your favorites. My mother made this often for weeknight meals and to serve to guests. It has now become one of my favorites for entertaining. Whenever I make this for friends who haven't tried it, they always request it when they come over again.

8 boneless skinless
   chicken thighs

2 tablespoons (30 g)
   unsalted butter

1 teaspoon extra-virgin olive oil

1 medium yellow onion,
   finely diced

2 garlic cloves, minced

¼ teaspoon crushed red
   pepper flakes

¼ teaspoon nutmeg

¼ teaspoon cinnamon

1 cup (240 ml) red wine

1 tablespoon tomato paste

3 cups (300 ml) hot water

2 teaspoons kosher salt

2 cups (225 g) dried orzo

Preheat the oven to 350°F (180°C). Pat the chicken dry using paper towels.

In a Dutch oven, melt the butter with the oil over medium-high heat. Add the chicken thighs (top side down) and sear on one side only for 3 to 4 minutes until golden brown. Remove the chicken and set aside.

Reduce the heat to medium. Add the onion to the pot and sauté for 3 to 4 minutes until tender. Stir in the garlic, red pepper flakes, nutmeg, and cinnamon, and sauté for an additional 2 minutes.

Pour in the red wine and simmer until it has reduced by half, 4 to 5 minutes. Stir in the tomato paste, hot water, and salt.

Pour in the orzo and spread it evenly over the bottom of the pot. Gently nestle the chicken (browned side up) into the orzo. Bring to a simmer.

Remove from the heat, cover with a lid or aluminum foil, and bake in the oven for 20 to 25 minutes until the orzo and chicken are cooked through.

PILESHKI
CHICKEN PIE
MUSAKA

My sister calls this "the recipe to make when you're not sure what to make." It is so easy to put together and makes great leftovers. The sour cream really adds another dimension of flavor and richness to the chicken. It is one of our favorite comfort food dishes.

2 lb (900 g) boneless skinless chicken breasts, cut into 1-inch (2.5 cm) cubes

1 teaspoon finely chopped fresh oregano

1 teaspoon finely chopped fresh thyme

2 tablespoons (30 g) unsalted butter

1 medium yellow onion, diced

1¾ cups (220 g), plus 1 tablespoon all-purpose flour, divided

½ teaspoon freshly ground black pepper

½ cup (125 ml) whole milk

5 eggs, whisked

2 cups (480 ml) sour cream

1 tablespoon extra-virgin olive oil, plus extra for greasing

Kosher salt

Preheat the oven to 375°F (190°C). Grease a 9- by 13-inch (23 by 33 cm) baking dish with olive oil.

In a large bowl, combine the chicken, oregano, thyme, and 1 teaspoon of kosher salt.

In a small sauté pan, melt the butter over medium heat. Add the onion and sauté for 3 to 4 minutes until tender. Pour the onion and butter into the bowl with the chicken. Toss to coat and set aside.

In a separate bowl, whisk together 1¾ cups (220 g) of the flour, 2 teaspoons kosher salt, and the black pepper, milk, and eggs until you have a smooth batter.

Pour the batter into the oiled baking dish to create a base. Scatter the chicken and onion mixture over the batter in a single layer.

Bake for 30 minutes until golden brown and cooked through. Remove from the oven and switch the oven to broil.

Mix together the sour cream, olive oil, and 1 tablespoon of the flour. Spoon the sour cream mixture over the chicken and broil for about 5 minutes until the top is golden brown and bubbling.

PILESHKI
CHICKEN & RICE
PILAV

We have a running joke in our family about my mother's devoted love of chicken and rice. There is something really homey about taking a large pot out of the oven and setting it on the table with the people you love around you. This dish is usually served with a selection of salads and Kisolo Mleko So Pechen Luk (Yogurt with Garlic, Cucumber, and Dill, page 31).

3-4 lb (1.5-2 kg) whole chicken, cut into serving-size pieces

½ teaspoon paprika

2 tablespoons (30 g) unsalted butter

1 large leek (white and light green part only), halved lengthwise and sliced

1 garlic clove, minced

¼ teaspoon crushed red pepper flakes

1 tablespoon tomato paste

1½ cups (280 g) long-grain white rice

3 cups (700 ml) boiling water

3-4 oregano sprigs

Kosher salt

Preheat the oven to 350°F (180°C).

Sprinkle the chicken pieces with 1 teaspoon salt and the paprika.

In a large Dutch oven, melt the butter over medium-high heat. Place the chicken (skin side down) into the hot butter and sear on one side only until the skin is golden brown, 5 to 7 minutes. Remove and set aside. Save about 1 tablespoon of fat in the pot and discard the excess.

Reduce the heat to medium. Add the leek and sauté until tender, 3 to 4 minutes. Stir in the garlic, 1 teaspoon salt, and the crushed red pepper flakes. Sauté for an additional 2 minutes.

Add the tomato paste and rice and stir for about 1 minute to toast the rice.

Pour in the boiling water and gently nestle the chicken pieces (skin side up) into the rice. Place the oregano sprigs on top.

Cover with a lid or aluminum foil and bake for 25 minutes or until the chicken and rice are fully cooked.

PILESHKO
POLNETO
SO PRAZI
STUFFED CHICKEN WITH LEEKS & CHEESE
SIRENJE

This dish looks so fancy and sophisticated but it is really quite easy to make. Leeks, feta, and ricotta is a common filling in Macedonian dishes, and the combination is delicious. The sweetness of the leeks is a perfect balance to the salty creaminess of the cheese. Toothpicks help to hold the chicken together in the oven. If you can't find skin-on boneless chicken breasts, ask your butcher to prepare them for you.

4 skin-on boneless chicken breasts (about 2 lb/900 g in total)

½ teaspoon kosher salt

¼ teaspoon paprika

1 tablespoon unsalted butter

1 teaspoon vegetable oil

FILLING

2 large leeks (white and light green parts only), diced

1 tablespoon unsalted butter

1½ teaspoons kosher salt

¼ teaspoon paprika

1 teaspoon fresh thyme

¼ cup (60 g) ricotta cheese

¼ cup (40 g) grated feta cheese

Preheat the oven to 400°F (200°C). Line a baking sheet with parchment paper. Carefully slice the chicken halfway through the breast to create a pocket.

Make the filling: In a large sauté pan, melt the butter over medium heat. Add the leeks, salt, paprika, and thyme. Sauté until tender, 3 to 4 minutes. Meanwhile, in a medium bowl, mix the ricotta and feta. Once the leeks are cooked, fold them into the cheese mixture and set aside.

Stuff each chicken breast pocket with a heaped spoonful of filling. Use a toothpick to seal the openings. Season on both sides with the salt and paprika.

In a large sauté pan, melt the butter over high heat and add the vegetable oil. Place the chicken breasts (skin side down) into the pan and sear for 3 to 4 minutes until golden. Then flip and sear the other side for 3 to 4 minutes.

Transfer the breasts to the baking sheet (skin side up) and roast for 10 to 12 minutes until fully cooked. Carefully remove the toothpicks just before serving.

PECHENA KOKOSHKA SO ZELKA I KOMPIRI

ROASTED CORNISH HENS WITH CABBAGE & POTATOES

*I love the delicate flavor of Cornish hens with wilted cabbage.
This recipe is so simple and rustic.*

2 Cornish hens, halved, backbone removed, wing tips trimmed

3 tablespoons (45 g) unsalted butter, melted

¼ cup (60 ml) olive oil

1 tablespoon kosher salt

1 teaspoon paprika

1 small green cabbage, cut into 2-inch (5 cm) chunks

4 medium potatoes, peeled and quartered

2 medium yellow onions, sliced into wedges

Preheat the oven to 400°F (200°C). Pat the hens dry with paper towels.

In a small dish, whisk together the melted butter, oil, salt, and paprika to make a marinade.

In a large bowl, combine the cabbage, potatoes, and onions. Toss with half of the marinade until evenly coated.

Place the hens in a separate dish and pour over the remaining marinade. Rub the marinade into the flesh with your fingers.

Place the cabbage, potatoes, and onions in a 9- by 13-inch (23 by 33 cm) roasting pan. Nestle the hens on top of the vegetables and roast, uncovered, for 35 to 40 minutes until the hens are cooked through and the potatoes are tender. Switch the oven to broil and, watching carefully, broil for 3 to 4 minutes to crisp up the chicken skin.

PECHENA PILESHKO I

BAKED CHICKEN WITH VEGETABLES

ZELENCHUK

This is a great meal for the summer months. As a young working mother, I love one-dish meals. My children love their vegetables sliced into rounds like little coins.

1 red onion, sliced

3 carrots, peeled and finely
   sliced into rounds

3 zucchini, finely sliced
   into rounds

3 garlic cloves, finely sliced

4 bone-in, skin-on chicken
   breast halves

MARINADE

¼ cup (60 ml) olive oil

1 tablespoon coarsely chopped
   fresh oregano

¼ teaspoon dried red
   pepper flakes

½ teaspoon paprika

Zest of 1 lemon

2 teaspoons kosher salt

1 teaspoon freshly ground
   black pepper

Preheat the oven to 400°F (200°C).

In a small bowl, whisk together the marinade ingredients.

In a large bowl, combine the onion, carrots, zucchini, and garlic. Pour half of the marinade over the vegetables and toss to coat. Spread the vegetables evenly in a 9- by 13-inch (23 by 33 cm) baking dish.

Place the chicken breasts in a large bowl and pour the remaining marinade over them. Toss to coat and place the chicken breasts (skin side up) on top of the vegetables in the baking dish.

Roast, uncovered, for 30 to 35 minutes until the chicken is cooked through and brown and the vegetables are tender.

Switch the oven to broil for 3 to 4 minutes, watching carefully, to crisp up the chicken skin.

PILESHKO SO PECHURKI

CHICKEN & MUSHROOMS

Many varieties of mushrooms grow wild throughout the regions of Macedonia. Cremini or button mushrooms are still among the most common cooking mushrooms, but the Boletus family mushrooms, found predominantly in the oak forests, are also widely used. It is the same variety as the porcini or penny bun mushroom and, if you can find them fresh (not dried and reconstituted), I highly recommend trying them in this recipe.

2 tablespoons extra-virgin olive oil

2 leeks (white and light green parts only), sliced into ¼-inch (6 mm) rings

2 garlic cloves, coarsely chopped

1½ teaspoons kosher salt

½ teaspoon paprika

½ teaspoon cinnamon

½ teaspoon freshly ground black pepper

4 cups (280 g) sliced Cremini or button mushrooms

1 cup (240 ml) red wine

1 cup (250 g) stewed or diced tomatoes (from a jar or can)

4–6 medium potatoes, peeled and cut into 2-inch (5 cm) pieces

6 boneless skinless chicken thighs, halved

Preheat the oven to 375°F (190°C).

In a large Dutch oven, heat the oil over medium heat. Add the leeks and sauté until tender, 3 to 4 minutes. Stir in the garlic, salt, paprika, cinnamon, and black pepper and sauté for an additional 2 minutes.

Add the mushrooms and cook, stirring constantly, for 5 minutes until they begin to soften. Pour in the wine and simmer until it has reduced by half, 4 to 5 minutes.

Add the stewed tomatoes. Bring to a simmer and fold in the potatoes so they are coated. Gently nestle the chicken between the potatoes and mushrooms in the pot.

Cover with a lid or aluminum foil and bake in the oven for 20 minutes. Remove the lid and bake for an additional 20 to 25 minutes, until the chicken is fully cooked and the potatoes are tender.

RIBA
Fish

Baked Whole Mackerel **161**
Pechena Skusha

Fried Fish Fillets **162**
Przheni Fileti Od Riba

Grilled Marinated Fish Skewers **165**
Marinarana Riba Na Skara

Broiled Fish with Lemon **166**
Riba So Limon

Stuffed Fish **169**
Polneti Riba

Baked Fish & Potatoes **170**
Pechena Riba So Kompiri

RIBA
Fish

Although much of Macedonian cuisine is heavily influenced by the Mediterranean, the country is geographically landlocked, so seafood like shellfish and squid are not part of the traditional cuisine. Instead, our fish dishes come from Macedonia's bountiful lakes and rivers, which are a source of freshwater fish such as trout, rainbow trout, and carp. Since these types of fish aren't always available in North American markets, I recreated these recipes using fish with similar flavors and textures.

PECHENA SKUSHA

BAKED WHOLE MACKEREL

This is a very traditional way to cook fish in Macedonia. In 2002, I traveled to my parents' villages with them for the first time. We visited my aunt and uncle's holiday home, where, overlooking the beautiful mountains and amid the tranquility of the land, we feasted on beautiful baked whole fish that was freshly caught from the lake earlier that day.

4 medium-size whole mackerel, cleaned and trimmed

2 tablespoons extra-virgin olive oil, divided, plus extra for greasing

1 medium yellow onion, finely sliced

2 garlic cloves, minced

¼ teaspoon crushed red pepper flakes

1 teaspoon freshly ground black pepper

1 cup (240 ml) dry white wine

½ cup (125 ml) warm water

1 medium tomato, peeled and diced

4 thin lemon slices

Kosher salt

Preheat the oven to 350°F (180°C). Choose a baking dish large enough for the fish to lay flat, and grease it with olive oil.

Rinse and pat the fish dry. Arrange the fish flat in the baking dish. Brush the skins with 1 tablespoon of the olive oil and sprinkle with ½ teaspoon of kosher salt. Set aside.

In a small sauté pan, heat 1 tablespoon of the olive oil over medium-high heat. Add the onion and sauté until tender, 3 to 4 minutes. Stir in the garlic, red pepper flakes, 2 teaspoons of kosher salt, and the black pepper. Sauté for an additional 2 minutes.

Reduce the heat to medium. Pour in the wine and simmer until it has reduced by half, 4 to 5 minutes. Add the warm water and simmer for an additional 5 minutes.

Pour the onion and tomato mixture over the fish, leaving the head and tail slightly exposed. Place one lemon slice on top of each fish.

Cover the baking dish with a lid or aluminum foil and bake for 15 minutes. Remove the lid or foil and bake for an additional 12 to 15 minutes, until the fish is cooked through.

PRZHENI FILETI OD RIBA

FRIED FISH FILLETS

This is one of my favorite ways to eat fish. Pan-fried fish is commonplace throughout Macedonia, and you can really use any fish you like. I love a meaty fish but a delicate fish would work just as well in this recipe.

1 cup (125 g) all-purpose flour

2 teaspoons kosher salt

1 teaspoon paprika

2 teaspoons dill, coarsely chopped, divided

4 firm white fish fillets, such as cod, halibut, bass, or haddock, skin removed

¼ cup (60 ml) vegetable oil, for frying

4–6 lemon wedges, for garnish

In a shallow dish, mix together the flour, salt, paprika, and 1 teaspoon of the chopped dill.

Coat each fish fillet in the seasoned flour and shake off any excess. Set aside.

In a large sauté pan, heat the oil until it begins to shimmer and reaches a temperature of about 350°F (180°C).

Carefully place the fish fillets in the oil and fry for 3 to 4 minutes on each side until golden brown.

Just before the fish is fully cooked, sprinkle the fillets with the remaining 1 teaspoon of chopped dill. Transfer the fish to a plate lined with paper towels to drain excess oil. Place the fillets on a serving dish and garnish with lemon wedges.

MARINARANA RIBA NA SKARA

GRILLED MARINATED FISH SKEWERS

These fish skewers are inspired by the street vendors of Macedonia's lakeside villages and towns. I love to make them with a selection of mezze dishes when friends are coming over in the afternoon. I keep them marinated and pre-skewered in the fridge and just grill a few at a time throughout the day as we relax and graze on various dishes. You will need 8 to 10 metal or pre-soaked bamboo skewers (soak bamboo skewers for 20 minutes).

1 garlic clove

¼ cup (6 g) fresh mint

¼ cup (6 g) fresh parsley

1 teaspoon kosher salt

½ teaspoon freshly ground
  black pepper

¼ cup (60 ml) extra-virgin
  olive oil

Juice of ½ lemon

2 lb (900 g) firm white fish
  fillets, such as halibut, bass,
  or swordfish, cut into 1-inch
  (2.5 cm) chunks

1 medium red onion, cut into
  1-inch (2.5 cm) pieces

In a blender, purée the garlic, mint, parsley, salt, black pepper, olive oil, and lemon juice to make a marinade.

Place the fish in a large bowl. Pour the marinade over the fish and gently toss to coat. Refrigerate for 1 hour to marinate.

Remove the fish from the refrigerator and alternately thread 3 pieces of fish and 2 pieces of onion onto each skewer.

Heat a grill pan or grill to medium-high heat. Grill the fish for 3 to 4 minutes on each side until golden brown cooked through.

Serve immediately.

RIBA SO LIMON

BROILED FISH WITH LEMON

This is a healthy, delicious way to enjoy any type of fish. I love to use large fillets of fish from my fishmonger. It is ridiculously easy to make and so impressive to serve. You can use any fish you like.

2 tablespoons (30 g) unsalted butter, melted

2 teaspoons olive oil, plus extra for greasing

1½ teaspoons kosher salt

½ teaspoon freshly ground black pepper

1 teaspoon finely chopped fresh parsley

Zest of 1 lemon

Juice of ½ lemon

One 2 lb (900 g) fillet black cod or other flaky fish

Grilled or fresh lemon slices, for garnish (optional)

In a bowl, whisk together the melted butter, olive oil, salt, black pepper, parsley, lemon zest, and lemon juice to make a marinade.

Grease a baking sheet with olive oil. Place the fish on the greased baking sheet (skin side down) and pour over the marinade. Cover the fish with plastic wrap and refrigerate for 1 hour.

Place a rack in the middle of your oven and turn on the broiler.

Remove the plastic wrap and place the baking sheet on the middle rack. Broil for 7 to 10 minutes until the fish is cooked through.

Garnish with grilled or fresh lemon slices.

POLNETI RIBA

STUFFED FISH

*I love the simple elegance of this whole fish with rice filling.
The presentation of the dish is just so beautiful. My Australian
husband fell in love with this recipe when I first made it for him.*

4 medium-size whole white
   fish, such as trout or mackerel,
   cleaned and trimmed
1 tablespoon extra-virgin olive oil

FILLING

1 tablespoon unsalted butter
½ cup (90 g) long-grain white
   rice, rinsed and drained
1 tablespoon extra-virgin olive
   oil, plus extra for greasing
1 medium tomato, seeds
   removed, finely diced
2 tablespoons finely
   chopped parsley
1 tablespoon finely
   chopped dill
Zest of 1 lemon
1 garlic clove, minced
¼ teaspoon freshly ground
   black pepper
Lemon wedges, for serving
Kosher salt

In a small saucepan, melt the butter over medium-high heat. Add the rice and stir for 1 minute until just toasted. Pour in 1 cup (240 ml) of water and ½ teaspoon of salt. Bring to a boil. Cover with a lid, reduce the heat, and simmer gently without stirring for 15 to 17 minutes, or until all the water is absorbed and the rice is tender. Turn off the heat and let stand, covered, for 5 minutes.

To make the filling, transfer the rice to a large bowl. Add the olive oil, tomato, parsley, dill, lemon zest, garlic, ½ teaspoon of salt, and the black pepper. Stir with a fork to incorporate. Set aside.

Preheat the oven to 400°F (200°C). Grease a baking sheet with olive oil.

Wash and pat the fish dry. Fill the cavity of each fish with about 3 heaped spoonfuls of filling. You can use a toothpick to seal the cavities of the fish, if you like.

Brush the tops of the fish with the olive oil and sprinkle them with ½ teaspoon of salt. Place the fish on the greased baking sheet and bake for 20 to 25 minutes until the skin has crisped slightly and the fish is cooked through.

Remove the toothpicks, if using, and serve immediately with lemon wedges.

PECHENA RIBA SO KOMPIRI

BAKED FISH & POTATOES

My children and nephews love this dish because the mild-flavored fish almost melts in your mouth. My grandmother used to make it for my sister and me when we were children, and now I love to make it for our children.

1 lb (450 g) medium Yukon gold potatoes, peeled

4 firm white fish fillets (such as sole, cod, halibut, bass, or haddock, 2 lb/900 g in total), skin removed

¼ teaspoon freshly ground black pepper

1 tablespoon chopped fresh oregano

Zest of 1 lemon

1 medium tomato, cut into ¼-inch (6mm) thick slices

1 tablespoon extra-virgin olive oil, plus extra for greasing

Kosher salt

Place the potatoes in a medium stockpot and add 4 cups (1 liter) of cold water and 1 tablespoon of salt. Bring to a boil over high heat. Reduce the heat to medium and simmer for 10 minutes. Drain in a colander and toss well to shake off excess water. Set aside to cool.

Preheat the oven to 400°F (200°C). Grease a 9-inch (23 cm) square baking dish with olive oil.

Cut the potatoes into slices ¼-inch (6 mm) thick. Arrange half of the potatoes in the bottom of the baking dish in one layer.

Arrange the fish fillets over the potatoes. Sprinkle the fish with ½ teaspoon of salt, the black pepper, half of the oregano, and half of the lemon zest.

Layer the tomato slices over the fish and arrange the remaining potato slices on top. Sprinkle with the remaining oregano and lemon zest and drizzle with the olive oil.

Bake uncovered for 30 to 35 minutes until the potatoes are golden and tender and the fish is cooked.

ZELENCHUK

Vegetables & Side Dishes

Traditional White Bean Stew 177
Tavche Gravche

Roasted Potatoes 178
Pecheni Kompiri

Rice Pilaf 181
Pilav Od Oriz

Fried Eggplants 182
Przheni Patlijani

Stewed Green Beans with Tomatoes 184
& Roasted Red Peppers
Boranja Barivo So Zarzavat

Cabbage with Dill 187
Zelka So Kopar

Fried Potatoes 188
Przheni Kompiri

Roasted Acorn Squash 191
Pechena Tikva

Potato Cakes 192
Kompir Kolachi

Roasted Vegetables 194
Pechen Zelenchuk

Pepper & Tomato Scrambled Eggs 197
Kaigana So Piperki I Domati

ZELENCHUCK
Vegetables & Side Dishes

Family meals in Macedonia are typically robust and usually comprise a multitude of dishes. Rich in agriculture, the land provides an abundance of fruits and vegetables, which have inspired a wonderful selection of vibrant dishes. Most of the ingredients are native to Macedonia, but over centuries of trade, a few nonnative ingredients have made a lasting impression. Rice has become an important part of the cuisine, a sign of the strong, enriching influence of the east.

TAVCHE

TRADITIONAL WHITE BEAN STEW

GRAVCHE

This is Macedonia's national dish, appearing on the table for weekday meals and celebrations alike. It is almost always served on Christmas Eve and for weddings and funerals. A simple dish of stewed beans and red peppers, it goes well with numerous meat, poultry, and fish dishes, but is just as good on its own with crusty bread. It is not fancy or extravagant, but captures the true essence of traditional Macedonian cuisine.

2 cups (370 g) dried white kidney or Great Northern beans, soaked for at least 6 hours in plenty of water

1 tablespoon unsalted butter

1 medium yellow onion, diced

1 red bell pepper, diced

1 teaspoon paprika

2 tablespoons all-purpose flour

4½ cups (1 liter) boiling water

1 tablespoon kosher salt

2 teaspoons chopped fresh mint

2 teaspoons chopped fresh parsley

Drain and rinse the beans and place them in a medium stockpot with 8 cups (2 liters) of fresh water.

Bring to a boil over high heat. Reduce the heat to medium and simmer, uncovered, for 30 minutes, until tender. Drain and set aside.

Preheat the oven to 375°F (190°C).

In a Dutch oven, melt the butter over medium heat. Add the onion, bell pepper, and paprika. Sauté until the vegetables are tender, 3 to 4 minutes.

Sprinkle in the flour and stir to coat the vegetables. Sauté for an additional 2 minutes.

Pour in the boiling water, salt, and beans. Gently stir and bring to a simmer. Cover with a lid or aluminum foil and braise in the oven for 1 hour.

Sprinkle with mint and parsley and bake, uncovered, for another 30 minutes. Serve hot or at room temperature.

PECHENI KOMPIRI
ROASTED POTATOES

Everyone in my family makes their own version of roasted potatoes. Although they are all delicious, I developed my own favorite way. I love a really crispy exterior and soft and buttery interior, with a hint of fresh lemon. To create my perfect roasted potatoes, I first parboil the potatoes to soften the interiors and "fluff" the exteriors prior to roasting. They go with any main dish in this book.

4-6 starchy potatoes, such as russet or Yukon gold, peeled and halved

3 tablespoons extra-virgin olive oil

1 teaspoon paprika

Juice of ½ lemon

Kosher salt

Preheat the oven to 400°F (200°C).

Place the potatoes in a large stockpot with 8 cups (2 liters) of water and 1 tablespoon of kosher salt. Bring to a boil over high heat, then reduce the heat to medium and simmer for 5 minutes.

Drain the potatoes and toss vigorously in a colander until they are dry and start to develop a fluffy exterior.

Transfer the potatoes to a heat resistant bowl. Toss them with the oil, paprika, and 1 tablespoon of salt. Transfer the potatoes to a roasting pan large enough to accommodate them loosely in a single layer.

Roast in the oven for 40 to 45 minutes, until golden brown and tender when pierced with a knife.

Remove from the oven and sprinkle the lemon juice over the potatoes just before serving.

PILAV OD ORIZ

RICE PILAF

Rice has an important role in Macedonian cuisine. Its mild character complements many of the salads and proteins. I'm a purist when it comes to rice. My grandfather taught me that first toasting the rice in a little butter and using boiling water instead of cold will keep the rice from sticking together, and it will cook perfectly every time.

3 tablespoons (45 g)
  unsalted butter
½ small yellow onion,
  finely diced
1½ cups (280 g) long-grain
  white rice, rinsed
  and drained
3 cups (700 ml) boiling water
1 teaspoon kosher salt

In a medium saucepan, melt the butter over medium-high heat. Add the onion and sauté for 3 to 4 minutes until tender.

Add the rice to the pot and stir for 1 minute until just toasted.

Pour in the boiling water and salt, cover the pot, and simmer for 15 to 17 minutes, until the water is fully absorbed and the rice is tender. Remove from the heat and let stand, covered, for 5 minutes.

Fluff with a fork and transfer to a serving dish.

PRZHENI
PATLIJANI
FRIED EGGPLANTS

This is a popular dish in restaurants in Macedonia. The Macedonian style of eating usually has lots of small plates and side dishes around a centerpiece of meat or fish. Fried eggplants are an important part of that tapestry.

1 cup (125 g) all-purpose flour

1 cup (115 g) plain dried breadcrumbs

3 eggs, whisked

1 medium tomato, seeds removed, finely diced

1 teaspoon coarsely chopped fresh mint

Zest of 1 lemon

2 medium eggplants, sliced in ¼-inch (6 mm) rounds

¼ cup (60 ml) vegetable oil

Kosher salt and freshly ground black pepper

Pour the flour into a shallow dish with 1½ teaspoons of kosher salt and 1 teaspoon of black pepper and stir to combine. In a second shallow dish, combine the breadcrumbs with 1½ teaspoons of kosher salt and 1 teaspoon of black pepper. Place the whisked eggs in a third shallow dish.

In a small bowl, toss together the tomato, mint, and lemon zest. Set aside.

Coat an eggplant slice in the flour, shaking off the excess. Then dip it into the eggs and shake off the excess. Finally, coat with the breadcrumbs. Repeat with the rest of the eggplant slices and set aside.

In a large sauté pan, heat the oil until it begins to shimmer and reaches a temperature of about 350°F (180°C). Working in batches, carefully place the eggplant slices into the oil and fry until golden brown, about 4 minutes on each side. Transfer the fried eggplant slices to a plate lined with paper towels to drain excess oil.

Arrange the eggplant slices on a serving dish and garnish with the tomato, mint, and lemon zest. Serve immediately.

BORANJA
BARIVO SO
STEWED GREEN BEANS WITH TOMATOES & ROASTED RED PEPPERS
ZARZAVAT

*These are typically served alongside meat or fish dishes, but I love them
on their own, too. I make this dish nearly every week, and I often double
the recipe to have some in the fridge. They make a fantastic lunch, served
cold with a chunk of feta cheese and a drizzle of olive oil. Sometimes I
add a diced potato or some mushrooms if I have them on hand.*

2 red bell peppers

2 medium tomatoes, peeled
and coarsely chopped

1 teaspoon tomato paste

2 tablespoons extra-virgin
olive oil

1 yellow onion, finely diced

3 garlic cloves, minced

¼ teaspoon crushed red
pepper flakes

1 cup (240 ml) red wine

2 lb (900 g) green beans,
washed and trimmed

2 teaspoons kosher salt

1 teaspoon freshly ground
black pepper

Roast the peppers over a grill or gas flame until the skins are completely
charred and blistered. Alternatively broil them in the oven (directly on the
rack, or on a baking sheet lined with parchment paper), rotating them every
15 minutes until charred, 30 to 45 minutes.

Place the peppers in a paper bag or heatproof container. Seal and let
stand for 20 minutes until cool. Peel off the skins and remove the stems
and seeds. Roughly chop the peppers and place them in a blender. Add the
tomatoes and tomato paste and purée for about 30 seconds. Set aside.

In a large stockpot, heat the oil over medium-high heat. Add the onion and
sauté for 3 to 4 minutes until tender. Stir in the garlic and red pepper flakes
and sauté for an additional 2 minutes. Pour in the red wine and simmer until
the wine has reduced by half, 4 to 5 minutes. Add the green beans to the pot.
Pour the tomato and bell pepper mixture over the beans and add the salt
and pepper. Using tongs, toss the beans in the sauce until evenly coated.

Reduce the heat to low. Cover the pot with a lid and simmer for 50 to
60 minutes until the beans are soft and the sauce has thickened.

ZELKA SO KOPAR

CABBAGE WITH DILL

This wilted cabbage is a perfect side dish with grilled meats, especially Kremenadli (Grilled Pork Chops, page 110). I love what happens to cabbage when it is cooked down in this way; it takes on an almost noodle-like texture.

1 tablespoon unsalted butter

1 medium yellow onion, sliced

1 garlic clove, minced

1½ teaspoons kosher salt

1 green cabbage, cored and thinly sliced

½ teaspoon red wine vinegar

2 teaspoons chopped fresh dill

In a large sauté pan, melt the butter over medium-high heat. Add the onion and sauté for 3 to 4 minutes until tender. Stir in the garlic and salt and sauté for an additional 2 minutes.

Reduce the heat to medium, add the cabbage, and sauté until the cabbage begins to wilt, about 10 minutes.

Remove from the heat. Stir in the red wine vinegar and dill and serve immediately.

PRZHENI KOMPIRI
FRIED POTATOES

These were our potato chips growing up. My father would make these for us as a late-night snack when we were watching a movie or playing board games. I highly recommend crumbling feta cheese over the top, which is my favorite way to eat them.

½ teaspoon kosher salt

½ teaspoon paprika

¼ cup (60 ml) vegetable oil, for frying

4–5 large starchy potatoes, such as russet or Yukon gold, peeled and sliced into ¼-inch (6 mm) rounds

Crumbled feta cheese, for serving (optional)

In a small dish, mix together the salt and paprika.

In a large sauté pan, heat the oil until it begins to shimmer, and reaches a temperature of about 350°F (180°C).

Working in batches to avoid crowding the pan, carefully place the potato slices into the oil. Fry for 3 to 5 minutes on each side until golden brown and cooked through. Transfer the potatoes to a plate lined with paper towels to drain excess oil, then sprinkle them with the salt and paprika.

Place on a serving dish and sprinkle with crumbled feta cheese, if desired.

PECHENA TIKVA

ROASTED ACORN SQUASH

There are several different squash varieties that grow in Macedonia, but acorn squash is among the most common. Growing up in Toronto, we were fortunate to have access to incredible squash. Acorn squash is one of my favorites. In Macedonia, squash is often prepared simply, roasted like this, or boiled and puréed as a filling for savory pastries. We only eat this in the fall when squash is in season and at its most flavorful.

2 acorn squash, quartered and deseeded	Preheat the oven to 375°F (190°C).
4 tablespoons (60 g) unsalted butter	Place the squash (cut side up) on a baking sheet.
½ teaspoon kosher salt	In a small saucepan, melt the butter and add the salt, cinnamon, and nutmeg.
¼ teaspoon cinnamon	
¼ teaspoon nutmeg	Brush the squash with the melted butter and roast in the oven for 45 to 60 minutes, or until easily pierced with a fork.

KOMPIR KOLACHI

POTATO CAKES

We loved to have these with saucy stews like Govedsko Meso So Kromit (Beef and Onion Stew, page 121). My mother would place one potato cake in the bottom of the bowl and ladle the stew over the top. Made a little smaller, these can also be served as mezze.

5–6 russet potatoes, peeled and cut into chunks

2 eggs, whisked

½ cup (60 g) all-purpose flour

½ cup (50 g) thinly sliced scallions

½ cup (75 g) grated feta cheese

1 teaspoon paprika

1 tablespoon finely chopped dill

¼ cup (60 ml) vegetable oil, for frying

Kosher salt

Place the potatoes into a pot of cold water with 1 tablespoon of salt and bring to a boil. Reduce the heat to medium and boil until cooked through, 7 to 10 minutes.

Drain the potatoes and set aside until cool and dry. In a large bowl, mash the potatoes or pass through a potato ricer until smooth. Add the eggs, flour, scallions, feta, paprika, dill, and 2 teaspoons of kosher salt, and mix until fully incorporated.

Form the mixture into patties about ½ inch (1 cm) thick and 2½ inches (6 cm) in diameter (or any size you like).

In a large skillet, heat the oil over medium-high heat until it begins to shimmer and reaches about 350°F (180°C).

Working in batches, carefully place the patties in the hot oil and fry for 3 to 4 minutes on each side, until golden brown.

Transfer cooked patties to a plate lined with paper towels to drain excess oil.

Serve hot.

PECHEN ZELENCHUK

ROASTED VEGETABLES

This is a simple medley of vegetables that grew in our garden. It is my go-to recipe for potlucks and large gatherings because it can sit at room temperature for a few hours. I often make a double or triple batch, just to keep in the fridge. The flavorful veggies make an excellent lunch with a chunk of feta cheese or a fried egg on top.

1 medium eggplant, peeled in stripes and cut into ½-inch (1 cm) chunks

3 medium zucchini, cut into ½-inch (1 cm) rounds

3 bell peppers (red, yellow, or orange), cut into 1-inch (2.5 cm) chunks

2 cups (300 g) cherry tomatoes, halved

2 large red onions, peeled and cut into ½-inch (1 cm) wedges

SAUCE

3 garlic cloves, peeled and coarsely chopped

1 tablespoon chopped fresh mint

1 tablespoon chopped fresh oregano

½ cup (120 ml) olive oil

1 tablespoon kosher salt

2 teaspoons freshly ground black pepper

Zest of 1 lemon

Preheat the oven to 375°F (190°C).

Make the sauce: In a blender, purée the garlic, mint, oregano, olive oil, salt, black pepper, and lemon zest.

Place the prepared vegetables in a large roasting pan. Pour the sauce over the vegetables and toss to coat.

Roast for 40 to 50 minutes until the vegetables are tender.

KAIGANA SO PIPERKI I DOMATI

PEPPER & TOMATO SCRAMBLED EGGS

This is a proper Macedonian breakfast. This recipe is so satisfying and can be spicy or mild depending on the peppers you use.

½ tablespoon unsalted butter

3 banana peppers, deseeded and sliced into ¼-inch (6 mm) thick rings

4 small tomatoes, diced

¼ teaspoon kosher salt

¼ teaspoon ground black pepper

8 eggs, whisked

¼ cup (40 g) grated feta cheese, for serving

½ teaspoon coarsely chopped fresh parsley, for serving

Sliced rustic bread, toasted

In a large skillet, melt the butter over medium-high heat. Add the peppers and sauté until tender, 3 to 4 minutes. Add the tomatoes and sauté for an additional 2 to 3 minutes. Stir in the salt and black pepper.

Pour in the eggs. Using a spatula, push the edge of the eggs towards the center, working your way around the pan until the eggs are just cooked. Transfer to serving plates.

Sprinkle with the feta cheese and parsley and serve with warm toast.

LEB
Breads

Braided Rich Bread **202**
Pogacha

Cornbread **205**
Pchenkarni Leb

Easter Bread **206**
Kozinak

Stuffed Crescent Rolls **208**
Polneti Kiflichki

Grilled Flatbread **211**
Pita Na Skara

Walnut Bread **212**
Leb So Orevi

Bread Rolls **215**
Poupchina

Sesame Rings **216**
Gevretsi So Susam

Filled Pastry **218**
Bourek So Sirenje

Filled Coiled Pastry **220**
Banitsa So Sirenje

Easy Filled Coiled Pastry **223**
Lesna Banitsa So Sirenje

Savory Pastry Fillings **224**
Bourek Plombi

LEB

Breads

Breads and baked goods are a most celebrated and important component of Macedonian cuisine. For my father, like for many Macedonians, bread is the fourth utensil, soaking up all the rich flavors of every meal. It is not just a staple of daily life; it also an important part of almost all celebrations, playing a symbolic role in wedding ceremonies, birth celebrations, baptisms, funerals, and Christmas, New Year's, and Easter traditions.

POGACHA
BRAIDED RICH BREAD

This is the bread of all breads in Macedonian cuisine. It plays a role in almost all of our most important traditions, including baptisms, weddings, and funerals. Traditionally, the bride and groom tear apart the Pogacha as part of their wedding ceremony—whoever gets the bigger piece is said to rule the household. But it is also an ideal day-to-day bread, and often portioned into simple loaves. My grandmother could make this bread using just her instincts to measure the ingredients.

½ cup (120 ml) warm water

2¼ teaspoons (7 g) active-dry yeast

¼ cup (50 g), plus ½ teaspoon white sugar, divided

3 eggs, divided

¼ cup (60 ml) vegetable oil, plus extra for greasing

4 cups (500 g) all-purpose flour, sifted, plus extra for dusting

2 teaspoons kosher salt

Sesame seeds, for garnish

Place the warm water in a bowl and add the yeast and ½ teaspoon sugar. Stir once. Cover the bowl with a plate and let stand until the yeast begins to foam, about 10 minutes.

In another small bowl, whisk together 2 of the eggs and the oil.

In a large bowl, whisk together the flour, salt, and ¼ cup (50 g) of sugar. Make a well in the center.

Pour the yeast and egg mixtures into the center of the well. Using a spatula, gently fold the flour into the liquid until incorporated and a dough begins to form. Transfer the dough to a lightly floured work surface and knead for about 10 minutes until it is smooth and elastic. Dust the surface of the dough with extra flour if it feels sticky.

Lightly grease a large bowl with vegetable oil and place the dough inside. Brush the top of the dough with a thin layer of vegetable oil. Cover the bowl with a large plate or tea towel and set aside in a warm place to rise for 1 hour, or until doubled in size. Grease a 9-inch (23 cm) round baking pan with vegetable oil and set aside.

Return the dough to your lightly floured work surface and divide it into 3 equal portions. Roll the dough into 3 ropes, each about 15 inches (40 cm) long and 2 inches (5 cm) thick. Attach the 3 ropes together at the top end and carefully braid them.

Coil the braided dough into a circle and place it in the greased pan. Tuck the ends of the braid under the coil. Brush the top of the dough with oil, cover loosely with a tea towel, and set in a warm place to rise for an additional 30 minutes.

Preheat the oven to 350°F (180°C).

Whisk the remaining egg and use it to brush the top of the dough, then sprinkle with sesame seeds.

Bake for 30 minutes, then reduce the heat to 275°F (135°C) and bake for an additional 15 to 20 minutes, or until golden. Let the bread cool before removing it from the pan.

When my husband and I got married, we had a small celebration in Toronto for family who wouldn't be able to travel to Los Angeles for our larger wedding the following year. My grandmother made us Pogacha, and I tore the largest piece. In LA, we found a local baker to make us a large decorated loaf. They took the "large" part literally and you could barely lift it! In this challenge, my husband won the bigger piece, but we joke that my grandmother's Pogacha is the only one that really mattered.

PCHENKARNI LEB

CORNBREAD

My grandfather always said this bread reminded him of the village. Corn grew well in my father's village and the stalks were used to feed the animals. The kernels were ground for bread, which was made weekly in wood-fired ovens (furna). It is similar in texture to American-style cornbread, but a bit less sweet.

1¼ cups (160 g) all-purpose flour

1 cup (120 g) medium-ground yellow cornmeal

¼ cup (50 g) white sugar

1 tablespoon baking powder

½ teaspoon kosher salt

1 egg

1 cup (240 ml) whole milk

1 tablespoon honey

4 tablespoons (60 g) unsalted butter, melted, plus extra for greasing

Preheat the oven to 375°F (190°C). Grease an 8-inch (20 cm) square cake pan with butter and set aside.

Sift the flour into a large bowl, and add the cornmeal, sugar, baking powder, and salt, and whisk to incorporate.

In another bowl, whisk together the egg, milk, and honey. Slowly mix in the melted butter.

Pour the wet ingredients into dry ingredients and gently whisk just until the flour is incorporated. Be careful not to over-mix.

Pour the batter into the prepared pan and bake for 30 minutes until golden brown.

Remove from the oven and let cool slightly before serving.

KOZINAK
EASTER BREAD

In the week leading up to Easter, my mother, sister, and I always made about 30 loaves of Kozinak. As per tradition, we wrapped each small loaf up with a few eggs (usually dyed red and yellow) and some chocolates, and gave one parcel to each of our neighbors, friends, and family members. In turn, we received multiple loaves from other families. Luckily, this bread freezes well and can be enjoyed for weeks after Easter. Its key ingredient is mahleb, *a spice that comes from the ground pit of a species of cherry tree called St. Lucie. If you can't find it, you can substitute vanilla extract.*

½ cup (120 ml) warm water

2¼ teaspoons (7 g) active-dry yeast

1 cup (200 g), plus ½ teaspoon white sugar, divided

5 cups (625 g) all-purpose flour, sifted, plus extra for dusting

½ teaspoon kosher salt

8 tablespooons (113 g) unsalted butter, melted

½ cup (120 ml) warm whole milk

4 eggs, divided

Juice of 1 medium orange

Zest of 1 orange

1 teaspoon ground *mahleb*, or 1 tablespoon vanilla extract

Vegetable oil, for greasing

Sesame seeds, for garnish

Place the warm water in a small bowl and add the yeast and ½ teaspoon sugar, and stir once. Cover the bowl with a plate and let stand until the yeast begins to foam, about 10 minutes.

In a large bowl, whisk together the flour and salt and make a well in the center.

In another bowl, whisk together the melted butter, milk, 1 cup (200 g) sugar, 3 of the eggs, orange juice, orange zest, and *mahleb* or vanilla.

Pour the melted butter and milk mixture into the center of the well. Using a spatula, gently fold the flour into the liquid until incorporated and a dough begins to form. Transfer the dough to a lightly floured work surface and knead for about 10 minutes until it is smooth and elastic. Dust the surface of the dough with extra flour if it starts to feel sticky.

Lightly grease a large bowl with vegetable oil and place the dough inside. Brush the top of the dough with a thin layer of vegetable oil. Cover the bowl with a large plate or tea towel and set aside in a warm place to rise for 2 hours, or until doubled in size.

Grease 2 loaf pans with vegetable oil.

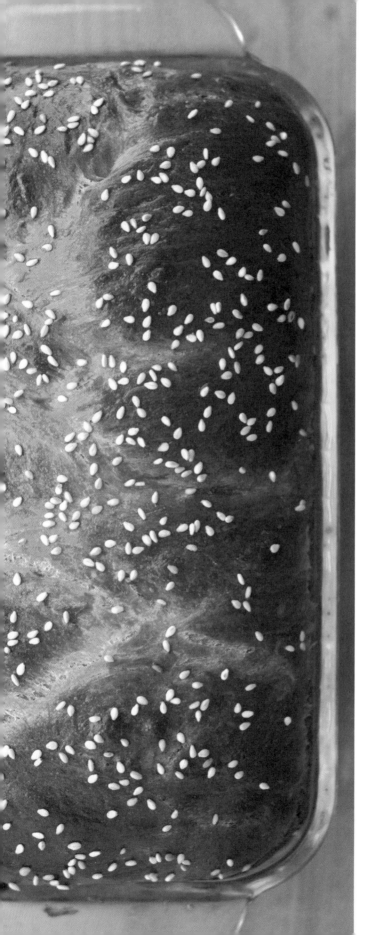

Return the dough to your lightly floured work surface and divide it into 6 equal portions. Roll each portion into a rope about 10 inches (25 cm) long. Attach 3 of the ropes together at the top end and carefully braid them. Tuck the ends of the braid under the loaf and place it into a greased loaf pan. Repeat with the remaining 3 ropes so you have 2 loaves. Brush the tops of the loaves with oil, cover loosely with plastic wrap, and set aside in a warm place to rise again for 30 minutes.

Preheat the oven to 350°F (180°C).

Whisk the remaining egg, and use it to brush the top of each loaf. Sprinkle the loaves with sesame seeds.

Bake for 25 to 30 minutes until golden brown and cooked through. Remove from oven and let cool for 10 minutes before removing from the pan.

POLNETI
KIFLICHKI

STUFFED CRESCENT ROLLS

My parents still live in the house where they brought me home from the hospital. Another Macedonian family lived next door, and we all grew up together. Every few months, a few of the Macedonian families in our neighborhood would get together for a meal, and my "aunt" Mitra next door made these better than anyone I know. I was fortunate to have her help with this recipe.

1 cup (240 ml) warm water

2¼ teaspoons (7 g) active-dry yeast

½ teaspoon white sugar

5 cups (625 g) all-purpose flour, sifted, plus extra for dusting

1 tablespoon kosher salt

1 cup (240 ml) warm whole milk

½ cup (120 ml) vegetable oil, plus extra for greasing

3 eggs, divided

FILLING

2 eggs

1½ cups (225 g) grated feta cheese

½ cup (120 g) ricotta cheese

¼ teaspoon kosher salt

Grease 2 large baking sheets with vegetable oil.

Place the warm water in a small bowl and add the yeast and sugar. Cover with a plate and let stand until the yeast begins to foam, about 10 minutes.

In a large bowl, whisk together the flour and salt and make a well in the center. In a separate bowl, whisk together the milk, oil, and 2 of the eggs.

Pour the yeast and egg mixtures into the center of the well. Using a spatula, gently fold the flour into the liquid until incorporated and a dough begins to form. Transfer the dough to a lightly floured work surface and knead for about 10 minutes until it is smooth and elastic. Dust the surface of the dough with extra flour if it feels sticky.

Divide the dough into 4 equal portions. Form each portion into a ball and place them on one of the greased baking sheets. Brush the tops of the balls of dough with vegetable oil. Loosely cover with a tea towel and set aside in a warm place to rise for 10 minutes.

Meanwhile, mix together the filling ingredients and set aside.

Roll out each ball into a circle 15 inches (40 cm) in diameter and about ¼-inch (6 mm) thick. Using a knife or a pizza cutter, cut the dough into 8 triangles.

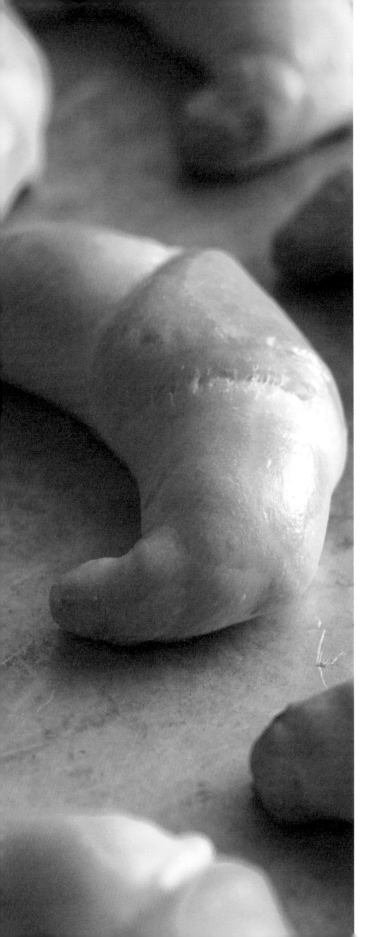

Place one triangle in front of you, with the wide edge closest to you. Place about 1 tablespoon of the filling on the wide edge. Fold the dough over the filling once and pinch the edges closed. Roll the dough up until the point of the triangle is wrapped over the roll. Gently pull the tips of the roll towards each other to form a crescent shape and place on a prepared baking sheet. Repeat with the remaining dough and filling, spacing the crescents about 2 inches (5 cm) apart on the sheets.

Brush the tops of the crescents with vegetable oil. Loosely cover the baking sheets with tea towels and set aside in a warm place to rise for 30 minutes.

Preheat the oven to 350°F (180°C). Whisk the remaining egg and use it to brush the tops of the crescents.

Bake for 25 to 30 minutes until golden brown (you may need to do this in batches if both baking sheets don't fit in your oven at once).

Best served warm. You can store them in an airtight container in the refrigerator for up to 2 days, or the freezer for up to 2 months. Reheat before serving.

PITA NA SKARA

GRILLED FLATBREAD

Along with Pogacha (Braided Rich Bread, page 202), pita is our most common daily bread, and almost always served alongside mezze, especially with dips. I make these grilled flatbreads a few times a week since my children love them. Freshly made, they go well with nearly everything.

2¼ teaspoons (7 g) active-dry yeast

½ teaspoon white sugar

1½ cups (350 ml) warm water

4 cups (500 g) all-purpose flour, sifted, plus extra for dusting

2 teaspoons kosher salt

3 tablespoons extra-virgin olive oil, plus extra for greasing

Place the warm water in a small bowl and add the yeast and sugar. Cover the bowl with a plate and let stand until the yeast begins to foam, about 10 minutes.

In a large bowl, whisk together the flour and salt and make a well in the center. Pour the yeast mixture and 3 tablespoons of olive oil into the center of the well. Using a spatula, gently fold the flour into the liquid until incorporated and a dough begins to form. Transfer the dough to a lightly floured work surface and knead for about 10 minutes until it is smooth and elastic. Dust the surface with extra flour if the dough starts to feel sticky.

Lightly grease a large bowl with vegetable oil and place the dough inside. Brush the top of the dough with a thin layer of vegetable oil. Cover the bowl with a large plate or tea towel and set aside in a warm place to rise for 1 hour, or until doubled in size.

Return the dough to your work surface and divide into 16 equal portions. Using your hands, work them into rounds about ½ inch (1 cm) thick and 8 inches (20 cm) in diameter. Use a rolling pin if you want the breads to be thinner.

Heat a grill pan over medium-high heat and brush with olive oil. Place a dough round on the pan and cook for 2 to 3 minutes on each side until the grill marks are golden brown. Repeat with the remaining dough, brushing the grill pan with olive oil between each batch.

These are best served fresh, but you can freeze them for up to 2 months and reheat as needed.

LEB SO OREVI
WALNUT BREAD

This bread is hearty and comforting. One of my favorite breakfasts is a few toasted slices of walnut bread with butter and jam and a steaming cup of planenski chai *(mountain tea), made from a flower similar to chamomile that grows wild in the mountains of Macedonia.*

1½ cups (350 ml) warm water

2 teaspoons (6 g) active-dry yeast

½ teaspoon white sugar

¼ cup (60 ml) honey

2 tablespoons extra-virgin olive oil, plus extra for greasing

4 cups (500 g) all-purpose flour, sifted, plus extra for dusting

2 teaspoons kosher salt

2 cups (240 g) coarsely chopped walnuts

8 walnut halves, for garnish

Place the warm water in a small bowl and stir in the yeast and sugar. Cover the bowl with a plate and let stand until the yeast begins to foam, 10 minutes.

In another small bowl, whisk together the honey and oil.

In a large bowl, mix together the flour, salt, and chopped walnuts. Make a well in the center. Pour the yeast mixture and the honey mixture into the center of the well. Using a spatula, gently fold the flour into the liquid until incorporated and a dough begins to form. Transfer the dough to a lightly floured work surface and knead for about 10 minutes until it is smooth and elastic. Dust the surface with extra flour if the dough starts to feel sticky.

Lightly grease a large bowl with vegetable oil and place the dough inside. Brush the top of the dough with a thin layer of vegetable oil. Cover the bowl with a large plate or tea towel and set aside in a warm place to rise for 1 hour, or until doubled in size.

Preheat the oven to 400°F (200°C). Grease a baking sheet with olive oil.

Return the dough to your work surface and gently shape it into a log about 18 inches (45 cm) long, being careful not to overwork the dough. Mold the dough into a ring about 9 inches (23 cm) in diameter, leaving a hole in the center, and place the ring on the baking sheet. Press evenly spaced walnut halves into the top of the dough.

Bake for 10 minutes, then reduce the heat to 350°F (180°C) and bake for an additional 40 minutes, until golden brown. It should have a crisp, hearty crust and a rich, dense interior.

POUPCHINA
BREAD ROLLS

Soft and airy, these little buns make great dinner rolls or sandwich bread.

½ cup (120 ml) warm water

2¼ teaspoons (7 g)
active-dry yeast

3 tablespoons, plus
½ teaspoon white sugar,
divided

½ cup (120 ml) whole milk

4 tablespoons (60 g)
unsalted butter

2 eggs, whisked

4 cups (500 g) all-purpose
flour, sifted, plus extra
for dusting

1 teaspoon kosher salt

Vegetable oil for greasing

Place the warm water in a small bowl, add the yeast and ½ teaspoon of the sugar, and stir once. Cover the bowl with a plate and let stand until the yeast begins to foam, about 10 minutes.

In a small saucepan, bring the milk and butter to a simmer. Remove from the heat and set aside to cool until warm.

Place the eggs in a small bowl and, whisking constantly, slowly pour the milk and butter mixture into the eggs.

In a large bowl, combine the flour, salt, and the 3 tablespoons of sugar. Make a well in the center. Pour the yeast mixture and egg mixture into the center of the well. Using a spatula, gently fold the flour into the liquid until incorporated and a dough begins to form. Transfer the dough to a lightly floured work surface and knead for about 10 minutes until smooth and elastic. Dust the surface with extra flour if the dough starts to feel sticky.

Lightly grease a large bowl with vegetable oil and place the dough inside. Brush the top of the dough with a thin layer of vegetable oil. Cover the bowl with a large plate or tea towel and set aside in a warm place to rise for 1 hour, or until doubled in size.

Grease a baking sheet with oil. Divide the dough into 8 equal portions. Form each portion into a smooth ball and place on the greased baking sheet. Brush each ball with oil. Loosely cover the baking sheet with a tea towel and set aside in a warm place to rise for an additional 30 minutes.

Preheat the oven to 350°F (180°C). Remove the plastic wrap. Dust the tops of the dough with a little flour and bake for 20 minutes until golden brown. The rolls should be soft and fluffy.

GEVRETSI SO SUSAM

SESAME RINGS

MAKES 16

These are much coveted, especially in the Kavadarci region of Macedonia. When we were children attending Macedonian language school, there was a lovely old man who sold them outside of the school, and we always stopped to have one. They are common in Macedonian bakeries and are popular as an afternoon snack.

MACEDONIA

216

¾ cup (180 ml) warm water
1 teaspoon (3 g) active-dry yeast
2 tablespoons, plus ½ teaspoon sugar, divided
3 cups (375 g) all-purpose flour, sifted, plus extra for dusting
2 teaspoons kosher salt
2 tablespoons extra-virgin olive oil, plus extra for greasing
2 egg whites, whisked
1 cup (145 g) sesame seeds

Place the warm water in a small bowl, add the yeast and ½ teaspoon sugar, and stir once. Cover the bowl with a plate and let stand until the yeast begins to foam, about 10 minutes.

In a large bowl, combine the flour, salt, and the 2 tablespoons of sugar. Make a well in the center.

Pour the yeast mixture and 2 tablespoons of olive oil into the center of the well. Using a spatula, gently fold the flour into the liquid until incorporated and a dough begins to form. Transfer the dough to a lightly floured work surface and knead for about 10 minutes until it is smooth and elastic. Dust the surface with extra flour if the dough starts to feel sticky.

Lightly grease a large bowl with vegetable oil and place the dough inside. Brush the top of the dough with a thin layer of olive oil. Cover the bowl with a large plate or tea towel and set aside in a warm place to rise for 1 hour, until doubled in size.

Preheat the oven to 375°F (190°C). Grease 2 baking sheets with olive oil.

Transfer the dough to a clean work surface and divide it into 16 equal portions. Roll each portion into a log about ½-inch (1 cm) thick and 8 inches (20 cm) long.

Connect the ends of each log to form a ring. Place the rings on the greased baking sheets, spacing them 2 inches (5 cm) apart, and cover loosely with a tea towel. Set aside in a warm place to rise again for 30 minutes.

Brush each ring with the whisked egg whites and cover generously with sesame seeds.

Bake for 25 to 30 minutes until golden brown. (You may need to bake in batches if both baking sheets do not fit in your oven at once.)

BOUREK
FILLED PASTRY

Bourek is an institution in Macedonia. This filled pastry is found throughout the different regions and is known by different names. Depending on whether it is the tray-baked or coiled style, it is sometimes known as pita, kora, zelnik, or maznik. I have included the classic cheese filling, but fillings vary as well—you can find a variety of filling options (Bourek Plombi) on page 224. The standard for a great bourek is a flaky, buttery crust and delicious filling.

1 cup (240 ml) warm water
1 teaspoon (3 g) active-dry yeast
½ teaspoon white sugar
3 cups (375 g) all-purpose flour, sifted, plus extra for dusting
¾ teaspoon kosher salt
8 tablespoons (113 g) unsalted butter, melted
Vegetable oil, for greasing

FILLING
1 cup (150 g) grated feta cheese
1 cup (240 g) ricotta cheese
¼ teaspoon kosher salt
2 eggs

Grease a 9- by 13-inch (23 by 33 cm) baking dish with melted butter. Also grease a large baking sheet with vegetable oil.

Mix together the filling ingredients and set aside in the refrigerator.

Place the warm water in a small bowl, add the yeast and sugar, and stir once. Cover the bowl with a plate and let stand until the yeast begins to foam, about 10 minutes.

In a large bowl, combine the flour and salt and make a well in the center. Pour the yeast mixture into the center of the well. Using a spatula, gently fold the flour into the liquid until incorporated and a dough begins to form.

Transfer the dough to a lightly floured work surface and knead for about 10 minutes until it is smooth and elastic. Dust the surface with extra flour if the dough starts to feel sticky.

Divide the dough into 8 equal portions and form each into a ball. Arrange the balls on the greased baking sheet, spaced about 3 inches (8 cm) apart, and lightly brush each ball of dough with oil. Loosely cover the tray with a tea towel and leave in a warm place to rise for 1 hour, until about doubled in size.

Preheat the oven to 350°F (180°C).

On your work surface, roll out 4 of the balls into 5- by 7-inch (13 by 18 cm) rectangles, each about ¼-inch (6 mm) thick. Brush 3 of the rectangles with melted butter and place one on top of the other. Place the fourth rectangle on top. Do not brush the top of the stack with butter.

On a lightly floured surface, use a rolling pin to roll the stack out to ¼-inch (6 mm) thick, and about 2 inches (5 cm) larger than the bottom of your baking dish. Place the dough into the baking dish, with the edges hanging over the sides. Brush the top of the dough with melted butter. Spread the filling evenly on top, then fold in the edges of the dough over the filling.

Roll and stretch out one of the remaining balls of dough as thinly as you can, so it is just larger than the size of the baking dish. The dough should be almost transparent. Place this loosely over the top of the filling in the baking dish. Gently brush the top of the dough with butter. Repeat with the remaining 3 balls of dough, brushing the top of each layer with butter (including the top layer).

Bake for 40 to 50 minutes until golden brown and heated through. Allow to cool for 10 minutes before slicing it into squares.

BANITSA SO SIRENJE

FILLED COILED PASTRY

This is a traditionally Macedonian style of savory pastry. The filled pastry is shaped into a coil and sliced like a pie. The cheese filling is most common, but you can find many other fillings on page 224.

1 cup (240 ml) warm water

1 teaspoon (3 g)
active-dry yeast

½ teaspoon white sugar

3 cups (375 g) all-purpose
flour, sifted, plus extra
for dusting

¾ teaspoon kosher salt

8 tablespoons (113 g) unsalted
butter, melted

Vegetable oil for greasing

FILLING

1 cup (150 g) grated
feta cheese

1 cup (240 g) ricotta cheese

¼ teaspoon kosher salt

2 eggs

Grease 2 large baking sheets with vegetable oil.

Mix together the filling ingredients and set aside in the refrigerator.

Place the warm water in a small bowl, add the yeast and ½ teaspoon sugar, and stir once. Cover the bowl with a plate and let stand until the yeast begins to foam, about 10 minutes.

In a large bowl, combine the flour and salt and make a well in the center. Pour the yeast mixture into the center of the well. Using a spatula, gently fold the flour into the liquid until incorporated and a dough begins to form.

Transfer the dough to a lightly floured work surface and knead for about 10 minutes until it is smooth and elastic. Dust the surface with extra flour if the dough starts to feel sticky.

Divide the dough into 6 equal portions and form each into a ball. Arrange the balls on a greased baking sheet, about 3 inches (8 cm) apart, and brush each ball of dough with a few drops of oil. Loosely cover with a tea towel and leave in a warm place to rise for 1 hour, until about doubled in size.

On your work surface, roll out 3 of the balls into 9- by 16-inch (23 by 40 cm) rectangles, each about ¼-inch (6 mm) thick. Brush 2 of the rectangles with melted butter and place one on top of the other. Place the third rectangle on top. Do not brush the top of the stack with butter. Set aside.

Repeat with the remaining 3 pieces of dough, so you have 2 stacks, each made up of 3 layers. Cover loosely with a tea towel and let the dough rest for 20 minutes.

Preheat the oven to 350°F (180°C).

On your work surface, use a rolling pin to carefully and patiently roll out each stack of dough as thinly as possible into a rectangle about 18 by 32 inches (45 by 80 cm). You can also use your fingers to help stretch out the dough. It should be almost transparent. Don't worry if it tears slightly—when you assemble the coil, the holes will not be noticeable. Place the dough horizontally with the long side closest to you.

Place half of the filling along the long side of the dough closest to you, about 1 inch (2.5 cm) from the edge. Fold the edge of the dough over the filling and roll it away from you into a rope. Curl the end and begin to wrap the rope around to form a coil. Carefully place the coil onto the first baking sheet. Repeat this process with the second piece of dough and place it on the second baking sheet.

Brush the top of each coil with melted butter and bake in the oven for 45 to 50 minutes, or until golden brown. (You may need to bake in batches if your oven can't fit both baking sheets at once.)

Allow to cool for 10 minutes before slicing into wedges.

LESNA BANITSA SO SIRENJE

EASY FILLED COILED PASTRY

I developed this recipe because, as much as I love the process of making Bourek (page 218) or Banitsa (page 220), it is a labor of love and I don't always have the time. I experimented with rolling out store-bought puff pastry dough very thinly with flour, and the result is as close as you can get to the homemade dough. Find alternative fillings on page 224.

16 oz (450 g) package puff
　pastry sheets, thawed
All-purpose flour, for dusting
1 egg, whisked, for egg wash
Vegetable oil, for greasing

FILLING

1 cup (150 g) grated
　feta cheese
1 cup (240 g) ricotta cheese
¼ teaspoon kosher salt
2 eggs

Preheat the oven to 350°F (180°C). Grease a 9-inch (23 cm) pie pan or oven-safe dish with vegetable oil.

Mix together the filling ingredients and set aside in the refrigerator.

Lightly dust your work surface with flour and use a rolling pin to roll out each sheet of puff pastry until it is ¼-inch (6 mm) thick, creating two long rectangles, each about 30 inches (75 cm) long and about 12 inches (30 cm) wide. Slice each sheet of pastry in half lengthwise. You will have 4 long strips of dough. Prick the surface of each strip at random with a fork.

Brush the dough strips with egg wash. Spoon a quarter of the filling along the long side of one strip of dough, about 1 inch (2.5 cm) from the edge of the dough. Fold the edge of the dough over the filling and roll it up to create a rope. Repeat with the remaining strips of dough.

Using a bit of egg wash, gently pinch the ends of the ropes together to form one long rope. Form the rope into a coil and carefully place it in the pie pan. Brush the top with the remaining egg wash and bake for 45 to 50 minutes, until golden brown. Allow to cool for 10 minutes before slicing into wedges.

BOUREK PLOMBI
SAVORY PASTRY FILLINGS

Using in-season ingredients is an important part of how Macedonians cook. Savory pastries are made year-round with sirenje *(cheese) or* meso *(meat) fillings, but we typically use* pras *(leek) and* tikva *(pumpkin) in the fall, and* spanak *(spinach) and* kisela zelka *(sauerkraut) in the winter. These fillings can all be used for any of the savory pastry dishes on pages 218-223. Each filling recipe is enough for one Bourek (Filled Pastry, page 218), Banitsa (Filled Coiled Pastry, page 220), or Lesna Banitsa (Easy Filled Coiled Pastry, page 223). I recommend trying them all.*

Spanak SPINACH

1 tablespoon unsalted butter
3 cups (100 g) coarsely chopped baby spinach
Generous 1 cup (170 g) grated feta cheese
½ cup (120 g) ricotta cheese
1 egg
¼ teaspoon kosher salt

In a large sauté pan, melt the butter and add the spinach. Toss to coat, just until the spinach begins to wilt and has turned bright green. Then immediately remove from the heat, and mix with the remaining ingredients. Refrigerate until needed.

Kisela Zelka SAUERKRAUT

1 tablespoon unsalted butter
Two 8 oz (225 g) cans of sauerkraut,
   rinsed and drained
¼ teaspoon paprika
¾ cup (115 g) grated feta cheese
1 egg

In a medium skillet, melt the butter and sauté the sauerkraut with the paprika for 3 minutes until the liquid has evaporated. Remove from the heat and mix in the cheese and egg until fully incorporated. Refrigerate until needed.

Tikva PUMPKIN OR SQUASH

2–3 lb (1–1.5 kg) sugar pumpkin
   or squash, cut into 8 slices,
   seeds removed
½ cup (120 g) ricotta cheese
1 egg
½ teaspoon kosher salt
⅛ teaspoon nutmeg

Preheat the oven to 400°F (200°C).

Place the pumpkin slices on a baking sheet and bake in oven for 30 to 40 minutes, until fork-tender. Remove and let cool. Peel off the skins and place the pumpkin flesh in a food processor. Purée until smooth.

Mix in the remaining ingredients until fully incorporated. Refrigerate until needed.

Pras LEEK

2 leeks (white and light green
   parts only), finely sliced
1 tablespoon unsalted butter
Generous 1 cup (170 g) grated feta cheese
½ cup (120 g) ricotta cheese
1 egg
¼ teaspoon kosher salt
⅛ teaspoon finely ground
   black pepper

In a medium sauté pan, melt the butter and sauté the leeks for 3 to 4 minutes until translucent.

Remove from the heat and mix in the remaining ingredients until fully incorporated. Refrigerate until needed.

Meleno Meso GROUND MEAT

1 teaspoon extra-virgin olive oil
½ lb (225 g) lean ground beef
½ lb (225 g) lean ground pork
1 small onion, finely diced
½ red or green bell pepper,
   finely diced
1 teaspoon kosher salt
½ teaspoon paprika
½ cup (125 g) stewed tomatoes
   (jarred or canned)

Heat the oil in a large pan and brown the ground meats, stirring constantly for about 4 minutes. Transfer the meat to a plate and drain the excess oil from the pan.

In the same pan, sauté the onion and pepper over high heat until tender, about 5 minutes. Stir in the salt and paprika and toss to coat. Add the stewed tomatoes and return the meat to the pan. Reduce the heat to medium and simmer for 5 minutes. Allow to cool before using, or refrigerate until needed.

SLATKO

Sweets

Filo & Walnut Pastry   **231**
Baklava

Sour Cream Cake   **233**
Torta So Kiselo Mleko

Pear Strudel   **234**
Shtrudla So Krushi

Shredded Filo & Almond Pastry   **237**
Kadaif

Fritters   **238**
Pitulitsi

Sesame Cookies   **241**
Susamliji

Rice Pudding   **242**
Sutlijach

Almond Cookies   **245**
Badem Kolatsi

Yogurt Cake   **247**
Jogurt Torta

Syrup Cake   **248**
Ravanija

Syrup Doughnuts   **251**
Tulumbi

SLATKO

Sweets

Many of Macedonia's classic desserts are heavily influenced by the legacy of the Ottoman Empire. Honey, nuts, orange, and cinnamon are common flavorings. Macedonian sweets are not very complicated to make, and generally go very well with slivovitz (plum brandy), or planenski chai (mountain tea), a robust chamomile-like tea sourced from the mountains of Macedonia.

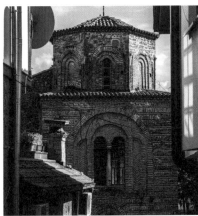

BAKLAVA
FILO & WALNUT PASTRY

Baklava can be found throughout the Balkan Peninsula, as well as in Greece, Turkey, Armenia, and the Middle East. The ingredients vary regionally, depending on what is available. Some use pistachios, pine nuts, or hazelnuts, flavored with cloves or rosewater. In Macedonia, baklava is traditionally made with walnuts and almonds, flavored with cinnamon, orange, and honey.

16 oz (450 g) package filo dough, thawed

FILLING
2 cups (200 g) walnut halves
1 cup (140 g) raw almonds
¼ cup (50 g) white sugar
2 teaspoons cinnamon
8 tablespoons (113 g) unsalted butter, melted

SYRUP
2 cups (400 g) white sugar
2 cups (480 ml) water
¼ cup (60 ml) honey
1 cinnamon stick
1 tablespoon fresh orange juice

Preheat the oven to 350°F (180°C). Brush an 11- by 15-inch (28 by 38 cm) baking pan with melted butter.

First, make the filling: In a food processor, combine the walnuts, almonds, sugar, and cinnamon and pulse for 15 to 20 seconds until the filling is coarsely chopped. Set aside.

Remove the filo from its package and immediately cover it with a damp tea towel. Make sure to keep the filo covered to prevent it from drying out.

Place 1 sheet of filo on a clean work surface with the long side in front of you. Brush the surface very lightly with melted butter and place another sheet on top. Repeat so you have a stack of 3 buttered sheets. Spoon a strip of filling along the long side of the filo stack, about 1 inch (2.5 cm) away from the edge. Fold the filo over the filling and roll into a long rope. Repeat this process with the remaining filo sheets and filling. Arrange the rolled ropes side by side in the buttered baking pan. Brush the tops of the rolls with butter.

Cut the uncooked rolls into serving-size pieces about 2 inches (5 cm) long, straight across or diagonally. It is important to cut the baklava before baking. Bake the baklava for 30 to 45 minutes or until golden brown. Remove from the oven and let cool for about 20 minutes.

In a saucepan, combine the syrup ingredients and bring to a boil. Reduce the heat to low and simmer for 15 minutes, until thickened. Let the syrup cool for 5 minutes before pouring it over the cooled baklava.

TORTA SO KISELO MLEKO

SOUR CREAM CAKE

This is my mother's signature cake. She made this often and the aroma that would permeate our home was heavenly.

1¼ cups (340 g) unsalted butter at room temperature, plus extra for greasing

1½ cups (300 g) white sugar

3 eggs

1½ cups (350 ml) sour cream

2¼ cups (280 g) all-purpose flour, sifted

1½ teaspoons baking soda

1 teaspoon baking powder

½ teaspoon kosher salt

1 tablespoon confectioners' sugar, for dusting

FILLING

¾ cup (100 g) light brown sugar

2 teaspoons cinnamon

½ cup (100 g) finely chopped walnuts

Preheat the oven to 350°F (180°C). Grease a bundt or angel food cake pan with butter.

Using a stand mixer with the paddle attachment, or in a large bowl with a hand mixer on medium speed, combine the butter and sugar until fluffy, about 4 minutes. Whisk in the eggs and sour cream.

In a separate bowl, combine the flour, baking soda, baking powder, and salt.

Slowly mix the dry ingredients into the wet ingredients, mixing at medium speed until fully incorporated, about 2 minutes. You should have a thick batter.

In a separate bowl, combine all the filling ingredients.

Pour half of the cake batter into the pan and smooth the top with a spatula. Sprinkle the walnut filling on top in an even layer. Spoon the remaining batter on top of the filling, carefully smoothing the top with a spatula.

Bake for 45 minutes, until a tester inserted into the center comes out clean.

Allow to cool in the pan for 10 minutes. Turn out onto a serving plate, and let cool for an additional 10 minutes, before dusting with confectioners' sugar.

SHTRUDLA SO KRUSHI

PEAR STRUDEL

This strudel can be made with any stewed fruit, like apples, cherries, or plums, but my mother has always made it with pears. The sour cream might seem unusual, but I find it makes the pastry light and flaky.

DOUGH

3 cups (375 g) all-purpose flour, sifted, plus extra for dusting

1 cup (225 g) cold unsalted butter, grated

½ cup (120 ml) sour cream

1 egg yolk

1 whole egg, whisked, for egg wash

FILLING

4 tablespoons (60 g) unsalted butter

1 tablespoon flour

¼ cup (60 ml) brandy

½ cup (70 g) light brown sugar

¼ cup (40 g) chopped dried apricots

¼ cup (30 g) chopped walnuts

1 teaspoon cinnamon

½ teaspoon kosher salt

3-4 medium ripe pears, peeled cored and diced

1 tablespoon freshly squeezed lemon juice

In a large bowl, use your fingers to mix the flour and butter until it looks like coarse breadcrumbs. Use a spatula to fold in the sour cream and egg yolk. Lightly dust your work surface with flour and knead the mixture just until it comes together smoothly. Be careful not to overwork the dough. Flatten the dough into a rectangle about 5 by 10 inches (13 by 25 cm). Tightly wrap the dough in plastic and refrigerate for at least 2 hours or overnight.

When the dough has been chilled, preheat the oven to 350°F (180°C). Line a large baking sheet with parchment paper.

Make the filling: In a large sauté pan, melt the butter over medium heat. Slowly mix in the flour and stir until you have a paste (roux). Add the brandy, sugar, apricots, walnuts, cinnamon, and salt, and stir until the sugar dissolves. Fold in the pears, and simmer over medium heat for 5 minutes. Remove from the heat and add the lemon juice. Set aside to cool.

On a lightly floured surface, roll the dough into a rectangle 12 by 16 inches (30 by 40 cm) and ¼-inch (6 mm) thick. Brush the top of the dough with some of the egg wash. Place the filling in a thick line down the center of the rectangle. Fold each side of the dough over the filling, making sure the dough overlaps to create a seal. Carefully flip the strudel over and place it on the baking sheet, seam side down. Cut slits into the top of the dough about 1 inch (2.5 cm) apart and brush the dough with the remaining egg wash.

Bake for 25 to 30 minutes, until golden brown.

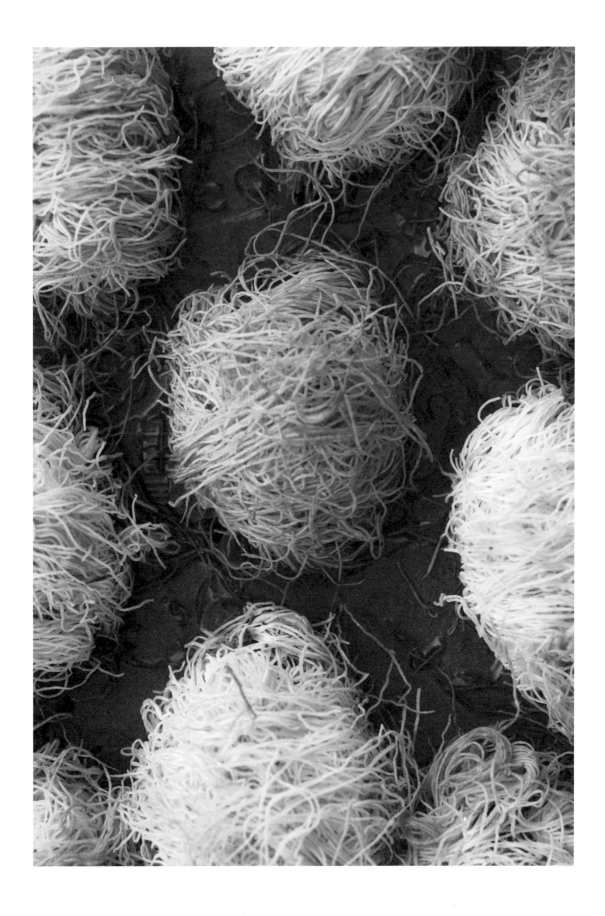

KADAIF
SHREDDED FILO & ALMOND PASTRY

The origins of this dessert lie in the Middle East, but it is much loved in Macedonia. It is crunchy, nutty, sweet, and so much simpler than it looks! I felt intimidated making Kadaif for the first time, but it really comes together quite easily.

1 lb (480 g) shredded filo dough (*kadaif*), thawed
8 tablespoons (113 g) unsalted butter, melted
Vegetable oil, for greasing

FILLING
½ cup (45 g) finely chopped almonds
½ cup (70 g) light brown sugar
¼ cup (30 g) plain dried breadcrumbs
1 egg, whisked
½ teaspoon cinnamon
Pinch of kosher salt

SYRUP
1 cup (200 g) white sugar
1 cup (240 ml) water
2 tablespoons honey
1 cinnamon stick

Preheat the oven to 350°F (180°C). Grease 2 large baking sheets with vegetable oil.

In a mixing bowl, combine the filling ingredients and mix well, making sure the egg is fully incorporated.

Place the shredded filo dough in a large bowl. Drizzle the melted butter over the dough. Using your fingers, carefully loosen and separate the strands and turn to coat them evenly with melted butter.

Pick up a handful of dough with your fingertips and place it in the palm of your hand in a nest. Place about a tablespoon of filling into the middle of the dough in your palm. Fold the dough over the filling and roll until the remaining ends of dough are wrapped around. Place the rolled *kadaif* onto a prepared baking sheet and repeat with the remaining dough and filling.

Bake for 20 to 30 minutes until the *kadaif* rolls are golden brown. You may need to bake in batches if your oven can't fit both baking sheets at once.

Meanwhile, make the syrup: In a small saucepan, combine the syrup ingredients and bring to a boil over high heat. Reduce the heat to medium and simmer for 5 minutes, stirring once, until the sugar has dissolved. Remove from the heat and set aside to cool slightly.

Remove the *kadaif* from the oven and set aside to cool slightly. Drizzle a spoonful of warm syrup over each *kadaif* roll. Serve warm or at room temperature.

PITULITSI
FRITTERS

These fritters are traditionally made for Christmas Eve, New Year's Day, or when visiting a newborn baby. They are a symbol of new beginning and new life. The dough itself is not very sweet, but a light dusting of powdered sugar adds just enough sweetness. They are best served fresh.

1½ cups (350 ml) warm water

2¼ teaspoons (7 g) active-dry yeast

1 tablespoon, plus ½ teaspoon white sugar, divided

4 cups (500 g) all-purpose flour

1 teaspoon kosher salt

2 eggs, whisked

4 cups (1 liter) vegetable oil, for frying

Confectioners' sugar, for dusting (optional)

Place the warm water in a small bowl and add the yeast and ½ teaspoon sugar. Cover the bowl with a plate and let stand until the yeast begins to foam, about 10 minutes.

Sift the flour into a large bowl and mix in 1 tablespoon sugar and the salt. Make a well in the center of the flour and slowly pour in the yeast mixture and the eggs. Whisk the ingredients together to form a batter.

Cover the bowl with a large plate and set aside in a warm place to rise for 30 minutes. Remove the plate and punch down the dough. Cover and set aside for an additional 30 minutes. Remove and gently punch down the dough again.

In a large pot, heat the oil until it begins to shimmer and reaches a temperature of 350°F (180°C). Working in batches so as not to crowd the pot, carefully drop spoonfuls of batter into the hot oil. The dough will float and expand. Fry for 2 to 3 minutes on each side, until golden brown and cooked through. Using a slotted spoon, transfer the cooked fritters to a plate lined with paper towels to drain excess oil.

Let cool slightly before dusting with confectioners' sugar. Serve immediately.

SUSAMLIJI
SESAME COOKIES

These are typically a celebration cookie and every Macedonian family I know makes them for special occasions. During the holidays, we always made platters of these cookies for our Macedonian neighbors and extended family.

5 eggs, divided
½ cup (120 ml) whole milk
½ cup (120 ml) vegetable oil, plus extra for greasing
1¼ cups (250 g) white sugar
1 tablespoon baking powder
¼ cup (60 ml) freshly squeezed orange juice
5½ cups (700 g) all-purpose flour, sifted, plus extra for dusting
¼ cup (40 g) sesame seeds

Using a stand mixer with the paddle attachment or hand mixer, mix together 4 of the eggs and the milk, oil, sugar, baking powder, and orange juice. Slowly add the flour, mixing for a few minutes, until fully incorporated and a dough forms. Shape the dough into a ball and cover with plastic wrap. Refrigerate for 20 minutes.

Preheat the oven to 350°F (180°C). Grease 2 large baking sheets with vegetable oil.

On a lightly floured work surface, portion out the dough into approximately 2-tablespoon-size pieces. Roll each piece of dough into a log about ½-inch (1 cm) thick and about 4 inches (10 cm) long. Fold each log in half and twist the ends together. Place the cookies onto the greased baking sheets, spacing them about 2 inches (5 cm) apart.

In a small bowl, whisk the remaining 1 egg to make an egg wash. Brush the cookies with the egg wash and sprinkle them generously with sesame seeds.

Bake the cookies for 15 to 20 minutes until golden brown. (You may need to do this in batches if your oven can't fit both baking sheets at once.)

SUTLIJACH
RICE PUDDING

This comforting dessert is almost effortless and full of flavor. Flavoring the milk with orange peel and cinnamon is the way my grandmother used to make it.

4 cups (1 liter) whole milk

1 cup (200 g) short-grain white rice

¾ cup (100 g) brown sugar

2 tablespoons (30 g) unsalted butter

¼ teaspoon kosher salt

1 cinnamon stick

1 strip orange peel, peeled using a vegetable peeler

3 egg yolks

Ground cinnamon, for garnish

In a medium saucepan over high heat, stir together the milk, rice, sugar, butter, salt, cinnamon stick, and orange peel. Bring to a boil and reduce the heat to medium. Simmer, covered, for 40 to 45 minutes, stirring often, until the rice is fully cooked. Discard the orange peel and cinnamon stick.

In a heat resistant bowl, whisk the egg yolks. Gradually ladle about 2 cups of the hot rice mixture into the egg yolks to temper the eggs.

Place the rice over low heat, and carefully pour the tempered eggs back into the pudding. Stir constantly for about 5 minutes.

Spoon the rice pudding into one large serving dish, or individual serving dishes or ramekins. Let it cool, then refrigerate until chilled. Garnish with a light dusting of cinnamon before serving.

BADEM KOLATSI

ALMOND COOKIES

There are many varieties of almond cookies made throughout the regions of Macedonia, but these are the style we made at home, particularly when we attended bridal and baby showers, where it is customary for guests to bring a dessert for the sweet table.

3 eggs

1 cup (200 g) white sugar

1 teaspoon vanilla extract

1 cup vegetable oil, plus extra for greasing

3 cups (375 g) all-purpose flour, sifted

2 teaspoons baking powder

¼ teaspoon baking soda

½ teaspoon kosher salt

1½ cups (140 g) toasted sliced almonds, divided

Preheat the oven to 350°F (180°C). Grease 2 large baking sheets with vegetable oil.

Using a stand mixer fitted with a paddle attachment or in a large bowl with a hand mixer, whisk the eggs. Pour in the sugar, vanilla, and oil. Mix at medium speed for 2 minutes.

In a separate bowl, mix the flour, baking powder, baking soda, and salt. With the mixer running at medium speed, gradually mix the dry ingredients into the wet ingredients. Mix just until fully incorporated and a dough forms. Using a spatula, gently fold in 1 cup (100 g) of the almonds.

Drop the dough onto the greased baking sheets in 2-tablespoon-size portions, spacing them about 2 inches (5 cm) apart, since they will spread. Carefully sprinkle a few sliced almonds over each cookie and press them gently into the dough.

Bake for 20 to 22 minutes until the edges are golden brown. Bake in batches if your oven can't fit both baking sheets at once.

JOGURT TORTA

YOGURT CAKE

This light and delicate cake is only mildly sweet, with a bit of tang from the yogurt, giving it a sophisticated flavor despite its simplicity. I almost always have the ingredients on hand, so I make it often for my young children. For entertaining, I often serve it with a dollop of Slatko Od Chreshi (Cherry Preserves, page 264) and a glass of slivovitz, plum brandy. I recommend serving this cake warm.

8 tablespoons (113 g) unsalted butter at room temperature, plus extra for greasing

½ cup (100 g) white sugar

2 eggs

1 cup (240 ml) plain full-fat Balkan yogurt (or any plain full-fat yogurt)

1 teaspoon lemon zest

1 teaspoon orange zest

2 cups (250 g) all-purpose flour

2 teaspoons baking powder

½ teaspoon baking soda

½ teaspoon kosher salt

Confectioners' sugar, for dusting

Preheat the oven to 350°F (180°C). Grease a 9-inch (23 cm) springform cake pan with butter.

Using a stand mixer fitted with the paddle attachment, or a large bowl and a hand mixer, cream the butter and sugar together until fluffy, about 4 minutes. Mix in the eggs, one at a time, until fully incorporated, about 1 minute. Fold in the yogurt and the lemon and orange zests. Set aside.

In a separate large bowl, sift together the flour, baking powder, baking soda, and salt. Carefully fold the dry ingredients into the wet ingredients just until a batter is formed. Be careful not to over-mix.

Pour the batter into the prepared cake pan, smoothing the top with a spatula. Bake for 30 minutes, or until the top is golden brown and a tester inserted into the center comes out clean.

Cool to room temperature. Remove the cake from the pan and dust with confectioners' sugar before serving.

RAVANIJA
SYRUP CAKE

The use of farina gives this cake an interesting texture and a mild flavor. Pouring the syrup over the cake when it is hot out of the oven allows the sponge to completely absorb the syrup, making this cake very moist and delicately sweet.

CAKE

6 room-temperature
   eggs, separated
¼ cup (50 g) white sugar
1 cup (180 g) farina
¼ teaspoon kosher salt
1 teaspoon vanilla extract
Butter, for greasing

SYRUP

3 cups (700 ml) water
1½ cups (300 g) white sugar
1 strip orange peel, peeled
   using a vegetable peeler
1 tablespoon orange juice
1 cinnamon stick

Preheat the oven to 350°F (180°C). Grease a 9- by 11-inch (23 by 28 inch) cake pan with butter.

In a large bowl, whisk together the egg yolks and sugar until they become a creamy light yellow. Fold in the farina, salt, and vanilla extract.

In a stand mixer fitted with the whisk attachment, or in a large bowl using a hand mixer, whisk the egg whites until stiff peaks form.

Carefully fold about one-third of the egg whites into the yolk mixture. Pour the entire yolk mixture back into the bowl containing the egg whites and gently fold until just incorporated.

Pour the batter into the greased cake pan and carefully level using a spatula. Bake for 20 to 25 minutes, until a tester inserted into the center comes out clean.

Meanwhile, in a small saucepan, combine all of the syrup ingredients and bring to a boil over high heat. Reduce the heat to low and simmer for 10 to 15 minutes, or until the mixture has thickened and reduced by about half. Turn off the heat and discard the orange peel and cinnamon stick. Set aside to cool for 10 minutes.

Remove the cake from the oven and immediately slice diagonally to create diamond-shaped serving pieces. Pour the hot syrup all over the cake and allow it to cool completely before serving.

TULUMBI
SYRUP DOUGHNUTS

These were one of the first things I wanted to eat when we traveled to my parents' villages—my father is from Rula and my mother is from Bresnitza. These mini doughnuts are made with a choux pastry, or pâte à choux dough. They are found in nearly every bakery in Macedonia. A pastry bag with a star-shaped tip gives the Tulumbi their unmistakable shape. Freshly fried, they are soaked in a flavorful syrup and are best served right away.

SYRUP

1 cup (240 ml) water
2 cups (400 g) sugar
1 large orange peel
¼ teaspoon kosher salt

DOUGHNUTS

1 cup (240 ml) water
8 tablespoons (113 g) butter
1 tablespoon sugar
½ teaspoon kosher salt
1 cup (125 g) all-purpose
  flour, sifted
3 eggs
4 cups (1 liter) vegetable oil,
  for deep-frying

In a small saucepan, combine all of the syrup ingredients and bring to a boil over high heat. Reduce the heat to medium and simmer for 5 minutes until the sugar and salt have dissolved completely. Remove the orange peel and set aside to cool.

In a medium saucepan, heat the vegetable oil over medium-high heat until it begins to shimmer, and reaches a temperature of 350°F (180°C).

In another medium saucepan placed over high heat, whisk together the water, butter, sugar, and salt, and simmer, whisking constantly, until the sugar and salt are completely dissolved.

Reduce the heat to medium-low. Using a wooden spoon, stir the flour into the saucepan and continue to stir until the dough forms a ball, about 1 minute. Remove the pan from the heat and whisk in the eggs, one at a time.

Transfer the dough to a pastry bag fitted with a star tip. Squeeze out 2-inch (5 cm) strips of dough into the hot oil, working in batches to avoid crowding the pan. Let them fry until golden brown, about 2 minutes on each side. Using a slotted spoon, remove the doughnuts from the oil and transfer to a plate lined with paper towels to drain excess oil.

Using a slotted spoon, dip the still-warm doughnuts into the syrup to fully coat them. Place on a serving dish and eat right away.

ZIMNICA

Preserves

Pickled Vegetables **257**
Turshija Od Zelenchuk

Dried Tomatoes **259**
Zachuvani Domati

Fig Jam **261**
Slatko Od Smokvi

Plum Preserves **262**
Slatko Od Slivi

Cherry Preserves **264**
Slatko Od Chreshi

Yogurt **266**
Jogurt

ZIMNICA
Preserves

Preserves are a very important element of the Macedonian table, and in Macedonia's past, a key part of survival. In the villages of Macedonia, storing food for the winter months was a communal family effort. Even during my childhood in Toronto, my family would get together every fall and spend a weekend working to preserve the fruits and vegetables grown over the summer. We used preservation techniques that were passed down through generations, and took pride in not being wasteful.

Homemade jams, eaten with breads and tea, are a popular Macedonian breakfast. Pickled vegetables are typically enjoyed in the evenings, with a glass of rakija (fruit brandy). Dried fruits and vegetables are common snacks or incorporated into recipes. Homemade yogurt is a staple as well, and my parents would make it once a week.

TURSHIJA OD
PICKLED VEGETABLES
ZELENCHUK

In the fall, my family spent weekends getting together to make preserves in preparation for the winter months. This medley of vegetables is great to have on hand, and we would quickly go through the jars. My uncle Zivko was the best in the family at making Turshija. As a child, this was the only way my parents could get me to eat cauliflower.

½ head cauliflower, cut into
   1–1½ inch (2.5–4 cm) florets
3 carrots, peeled, halved, and
   cut into 2-inch (5 cm) lengths
2 banana peppers (or use red
   bell peppers), sliced into
   ½-inch (1 cm) thick rings

PICKLING BRINE

1½ teaspoons brown
   mustard seeds
2 cups (480 ml) distilled
   white vinegar
6 garlic cloves, peeled
½ cup (100 g) white sugar
2 tablespoons kosher salt
1 teaspoon black peppercorns
¼ teaspoon crushed red
   pepper flakes

First make the pickling brine: In a stockpot over medium heat, toast the mustard seeds until fragrant, about 2 minutes. Pour in the vinegar and 1½ cups (350 ml) of water. Add the garlic, sugar, salt, peppercorns, and red pepper flakes. Increase the heat to high and bring to a boil.

If vegetables are to be consumed within 2 weeks, pack them in a clean jar or heatproof bowl and pour in the boiling brine to cover them fully. Set aside and cool, uncovered, until the brine reaches room temperature. Cover with a lid and refrigerate for at least 1 day before serving. Store in the refrigerator.

If preserving the pickles for longer-term storage, pack them into hot sterilized preserving jars. Pour in the hot brine leaving ½-inch (1 cm) headspace at the top. Using a skewer or a chopstick, poke the vegetables down into the jars to remove any air bubbles. Place clean lids on top and screw on the tightening rings.

Half-fill a large pot with hot water and place the jars upright in the pot. Pour in enough hot water to submerge the jars fully and bring to a boil. Boil vigorously for 10 minutes. Carefully lift out the jars and let them cool completely.

Check to see that the lids have sunk down tightly. Refrigerate any jars that have not sealed and use within 2 weeks. Store the sealed jars in a cool dry place for at least 1 week before opening. After opening, store in the refrigerator and use within 2 weeks.

ZACHUVANI DOMATI

DRIED TOMATOES

Tomato plants seem to just explode with ripe tomatoes all at once. My family's garden is always so bountiful with tomatoes in the last few weeks of summer. This is a great way to utilize an abundant harvest. They are great to snack on, or you can serve them as a mezze or side dish, drizzled with a little olive oil.

4 lb (1.8 kg) Roma tomatoes, halved lengthwise

1 bulb garlic, skin on, cloves separated and halved

¼ cup (60 ml) extra-virgin olive oil

2 teaspoons kosher salt

2 teaspoons freshly ground black pepper

Preheat the oven to 250°F (120°C).

Place all the ingredients in a large bowl and toss to coat.

Arrange the tomatoes on a large baking sheet in a single layer and roast for 2 hours. You may need to do this in batches.

Let cool and transfer to jars or a container. Store in the refrigerator and use within 1 week.

PRESERVES —

259

SLATKO OD SMOKVI

FIG JAM

Fig jam is a common Macedonian breakfast or snack, served with tea and bread or sometimes cookies. It also makes an excellent addition to cheeseboards. Growing up in Canada, fresh figs were not readily available, so my family almost always bought fig jam imported from Macedonia. When I lived in Los Angeles, I was fortunate enough to have a a beautiful mature fig tree in my backyard, and a fig tree was one of the first things I bought for our new home in Australia. Making this jam has become a yearly ritual I share with my daughter.

2 lb (900 g) fresh figs, stems removed and quartered

1½ cups (220 g) brown sugar

1 cup (240 ml) water

1 large lemon peel

1 large orange peel

2 cinnamon sticks

Juice of 1 lemon

1 teaspoon kosher salt

In large stockpot over medium-high heat, stir together all of the ingredients, then lower the heat and simmer gently until the mixture has thickened and the figs break down, approximately 1½ hours. Remove the cinnamon stick and citrus peels, and allow the figs to cool for about 2 hours.

Using a food processor or immersion blender, purée the figs to your desired texture. Return to the pot and place over high heat until the jam begins to bubble. Transfer to sterilized mason jars, leaving ½ inch (1 cm) headspace at the top.

Using a skewer or a chopstick, poke the fig jam down into the jars, removing any air bubbles. Place clean lids on top and screw on the tightening rings.

Half-fill a large pot with hot water and place the jars upright in the pot. Pour in enough hot water to submerge the jars fully and bring to a boil. Boil vigorously for 10 minutes. Carefully lift the jars out of the pot using tongs and let them cool completely.

Check to see that the lids have sunk down tightly. Refrigerate any jars that have not sealed and use within 2 weeks. Store sealed jars in a cool dry place. After opening, store in the refrigerator and use within 2 weeks.

SLATKO OD SLIVI

PLUM PRESERVES

These plum preserves are delicious as a sweet treat or as an accompaniment to cakes and breads. We often eat them straight from the jar or with a small drizzle of yogurt and chopped walnuts over the top. As kids, we also used to mix the syrup with sparkling water to make plum soda.

2 lb (900 g) plums, pitted
  and quartered
1 cup (200 g) white sugar
¼ cup (60 ml) water
1 cinnamon stick
2 strips of orange peel
¼ cup (60 ml) brandy

In a medium stockpot, stir all the ingredients together over medium heat and bring to a boil. Reduce the heat and simmer for 25 minutes until the plums are tender. Some of the skin may loosen from the flesh.

Using a slotted spoon, transfer the plums to sterilized jars. Pour the hot cooking liquid over the plums in the jar, leaving ½-inch (1 cm) headspace at the top. Using a skewer or a chopstick, poke the plums down into jars to remove any air bubbles. Place clean lids on top of the jars and screw on the tightening rings.

Half-fill a large pot with hot water and place the jars upright in the pot. Pour in enough hot water to submerge the jars fully and bring to a boil. Boil vigorously for 10 minutes. Carefully lift the jars out of the pot with tongs and let them cool completely.

Check to see that the lids have sunk down tightly. Refrigerate any jars that have not sealed and use within 2 weeks. Store sealed jars in a cool dry place. After opening, store in the refrigerator and use within 2 weeks.

SLATKO OD CHRESHI
CHERRY PRESERVES

Cherries are in season in the early summer in Macedonia and, like most fruits and vegetables, they grow in abundance. My parents have a thriving cherry tree in their backyard that my sister and I planted as children. These cherry preserves are sweet and tart with a bit of depth from the brandy. Spooned over yogurt, they make a great dessert or sweet breakfast.

6 cups (1 kg) sweet dark
　　cherries, pitted
½ cup (70 g) brown sugar
½ cup (100 g) white sugar
Juice of 2 lemons
¼ cup (60 ml) brandy
½ teaspoon kosher salt

In a medium saucepan, combine all of the ingredients and place over high heat. When the liquid starts to bubble, reduce the heat to medium and simmer for 1 hour, or until most of the liquid has evaporated and the mixture has begun to take on a thick consistency.

Transfer the cherries and their liquid to sterilized jars, leaving ½-inch (1 cm) of headspace at the top. Using a skewer or a chopstick, poke the cherries down into the jars to remove any air bubbles. Place clean lids on top and screw on the tightening rings.

Half-fill a large pot with hot water and place the jars upright in the pot. Pour in enough hot water to submerge the jars fully and bring to a boil. Boil vigorously for 10 minutes. Carefully lift the jars out of the pot with tongs and let them cool completely.

Check to see that the lids have sunk down tightly. Refrigerate any jars that have not sealed and use within 2 weeks. Store sealed jars in a cool dry place. After opening, store in the refrigerator and use within 2 weeks.

JOGURT
YOGURT

Many Macedonians, my parents included, make homemade yogurt every few weeks. The flavor and texture of homemade yogurt is so beautiful, and it contains no preservatives. Making your own yogurt may sound intimidating, but it is really quite easy. My father taught me to test the temperature with a finger: "If you can hold your pinkie in the milk for 10 seconds before it gets too hot, that's how you know it's ready." An instant-read thermometer takes away the guesswork.

6 cups (1.4 liters) whole milk
6 tablespoons full-fat
  plain yogurt

Pour the milk into a large saucepan and place over medium-high heat. Bring the milk to a temperature of 180°F (82°C) on an instant-read thermometer. The milk should be steaming, but barely bubbling. Be careful not to let it boil.

Carefully transfer the milk to a heatproof container and set aside to cool until the temperature reads 110°F (45°C).

Transfer ½ cup (120 ml) of the heated milk into a small bowl and stir in the yogurt. Add the yogurt mixture back into the container with the milk and stir to incorporate.

Preheat the oven to 200°F (90°C) and then turn off the oven.

Cover the heatproof container with a lid and wrap it in a towel to keep it warm. Place the wrapped container in the warm oven for 4 to 6 hours, without opening the oven door, until the yogurt has thickened.

Remove from the oven and refrigerate for a minimum of 2 hours before serving.

AUTHOR'S NOTES

If you think that you may have a food allergy or intolerance to any of the ingredients used in this book, it is a good idea to get specific dietary advice from your doctor or dietitian.

When preserving food for long-term storage, please consult the USDA *Complete Guide to Home Canning* for safe practices, and review the manufacturer's directions specific to your jars.

You can easily adjust the recipes to your personal taste. There are many variations to these recipes and different families and regions have their own adaptations.

All of the recipes in this book were created and tested using the following: kosher salt, extra-virgin olive oil, unbleached all-purpose flour, whole milk, large eggs, and homemade meat and vegetable stocks (if you use store-bought stocks, adjust the salt accordingly).

1 stick of butter = ½ cup = 113 g
1 tablespoon = 3 teaspoons = 15 ml

ACKNOWLEDGMENTS

Oliver Fitzgerald To my love: This was fun! Thank you for your patience and support through this entire journey. The memories of us starting this book in our tiny rental with the world's smallest oven in Los Feliz are some of my favorites. It was a time of creativity and joy. We worked hard on this and I'm so proud we saw it through. You and I shared so much in the creation of this book and in our life together. Thank you for indulging me on my every whim regardless how "out there" it was. You are my biggest supporter and I wouldn't want to live my life without you.

Linda Nitsou To my mother, Linda: I truly couldn't have created this book without you. Thank you for all your endless hours helping me with testing recipes, chopping ingredients, editing my thoughts, and consulting. It has been an incredible journey and you gave me the strength to see it through. I hope that I can be half of the mother to Kalina and Atteo as you have been to Christina and me.

George Nitsou To my father: Thank you for your devotion to us and ensuring we grew up to be educated women who had a strong understanding and connection to where we came from. Your never-ending thirst for knowledge is an inspiration to us and your guidance in the culture and historical background of Macedonia helped me immensely in writing this book.

Christina McIsaac Thank you for all your love and support. You are the strongest and hardest working woman I know. I would be lost without you and am so grateful that you are my sister.

Sophie Litsas Teta Sofa, your knowledge is like a portal from the old country to the new. You have guided me so much through the trials of this book. You helped me paint a picture of our heritage.

Hristina To my darling friend: you are a ray of sunshine in my life and I thank you for always cheering me on. You understand my determination and have never told me to slow down, but rather pushed me to be greater, which is always what I need to hear in times of doubt. Our friendship blossomed into family and I adore you.

Suzanna Bojadjieva Thank you for helping me connect to the stories and traditions of Macedonia. Thank you for broadening my knowledge; it has been a wonderful gift.

Dr. Christina Kramer, Professor of Slavic and Balkan Languages at the University of Toronto
Thank you for your work in helping me to ensure the translations in the book are accurate. You are beloved by the Macedonian community.

Meto Koloski, President of the United Macedonia Diaspora in the US Thank you, Meto, for your endless support and encouragement on the creation of this book. Your constant devotion to the culture and prosperity of Macedonians everywhere is truly an inspiration. I'm so proud of our friendship and proud of you, because your job at UMD is not easy, and you never waver in your determination.

Jake Rivera Thank you for your work on and support for this book. From our first meeting in Silver Lake you supported this project and were unceasingly patient until we got it just right.

INDEX

appetizers. *See* small plates

bacon
    Cabbage Rolls, 118–19
Baklava, 231
beans
    Pork Rib & Lima Bean
        Stew, 114
    Traditional White Bean
        Stew, 177
    White Bean Salad, 75
    White Kidney Bean Soup, 83

beef
    Beef & Onion Stew, 121
    Bite-Size Meatballs, 41
    Ground Meat Pastry
        Filling, 225
    Meatball & Rice
        Soup with Spinach, 84
    Meat Stew with
        Vegetables, 122
    Stuffed Grape Leaves, 42
    Stuffed Peppers, 112
Beet Salad, 57
bell peppers
    Roasted Pepper & Feta
        Cheese Dip, 38
    Roasted Red Pepper &
        Eggplant Dip, 27
    Roasted Sweet Pepper
        Salad, 61
    Stewed Green Beans with
        Tomatoes & Roasted
        Red Peppers, 184
    Stuffed Peppers, 112

breads
    Braided Rich Bread, 202–3
    Bread Rolls, 215
    Cornbread, 205
    Easter Bread, 206–7
    Easy Filled Coiled
        Pastry, 223
    Filled Coiled Pastry,
        220–21
    Filled Pastry, 218–19
    Grilled Flatbread, 211
    Sesame Rings, 216–17
    Stuffed Crescent Rolls,
        208–9
    Walnut Bread, 212

cabbage
    Cabbage Rolls, 118–19
    Cabbage Salad, 72
    Cabbage Stew, 106
    Cabbage with Dill, 187
    Roasted Cornish Hens
        with Cabbage &
        Potatoes, 150
cakes
    Sour Cream Cake, 233
    Syrup Cake, 248
    Yogurt Cake, 247
Carrot Salad, 71
cheese
    Easy Filled Coiled
        Pastry, 223
    Filled Coiled
        Pastry, 220–21
    Filled Pastry, 218–19
    Leek Crêpes, 47

Roasted Pepper & Feta
    Cheese Dip, 38
Stuffed Chicken with
    Leeks & Cheese, 148
chicken
    Baked Chicken with
        Vegetables, 153
    Chicken &
        Mushrooms, 154
    Chicken & Orzo, 142
    Chicken Pie, 145
    Chicken & Rice, 146
    Chicken & Rice Soup
        with Egg & Lemon, 88
    Chicken Skewers, 138
    Fried Skillet Chicken
        Breasts, 136
    Spiced Chicken, 135
    Stuffed Chicken with
        Leeks & Cheese, 148
cookies
    Almond Cookies, 245
    Sesame Cookies, 241
Cornish Hens, Roasted, with
    Cabbage & Potatoes, 150
Crêpes, Leek, 47
cucumbers
    Chilled Cucumber Soup, 81
    Cucumber Salad, 63
    Yogurt with Garlic,
        Cucumber & Dill, 31

desserts. *See* sweets
dill
    Cabbage with Dill, 187
    Yogurt with Garlic,

Cucumber & Dill, 31
dips
    Garlic & Walnut Dip, 32
    Roasted Eggplant Dip, 29
    Roasted Pepper & Feta
        Cheese Dip, 38
    Roasted Red Pepper &
        Eggplant Dip, 27
    Yogurt with Garlic,
        Cucumber & Dill, 31

eggplant
    Fried Eggplants, 182
    Lamb, Eggplant & Potato
        Casserole, 116–17
    Roasted Eggplant Dip, 29
    Roasted Eggplant Salad, 64
    Roasted Red Pepper &
        Eggplant Dip, 27
eggs
    Chicken & Rice Soup
        with Egg & Lemon, 88
    Pepper & Tomato
        Scrambled Eggs, 197

fish
    Baked Fish & Potatoes, 170
    Baked Whole Mackerel, 161
    Broiled Fish with
        Lemon, 166
    Fish Soup, 96
    Fried Fish Fillets, 162
    Fried Smelts, 44
    Grilled Marinated Fish
        Skewers, 165
    Stuffed Fish, 169

fruit

    Cherry Preserves, 264

    Fig Jam, 261

    Plum Preserves, 262

    Watermelon Salad, 68

garlic

    Garlic & Walnut Dip, 32

    Yogurt with Garlic,

        Cucumber & Dill, 31

Grape Leaves, Stuffed, 42

Green Beans, Stewed, with

    Tomatoes & Roasted Red

    Peppers, 184

Ground Meat Pastry Filling, 225

lamb

    Lamb, Eggplant & Potato

        Casserole, 116–17

    Lamb, Leek & Potato

        Stew, 109

    Roasted Leg of Lamb, 124

leeks

    Lamb, Leek & Potato

        Stew, 109

    Leek Crêpes, 47

    Leek Pastry Filling, 225

    Stuffed Chicken with

        Leeks & Cheese, 148

legumes. *See also* beans

    Lentil Soup, 87

    Split Pea Soup, 101

lemon

    Broiled Fish with

        Lemon, 166

    Chicken & Rice Soup

        with Egg & Lemon, 88

Lentil Soup, 87

Macedonian Mixed Salad, 53

meatballs

    Bite-Size Meatballs, 41

    Meatball & Rice Soup

        with Spinach, 84

meats. *See also* beef; chicken;

    pork

    Beef & Onion Stew, 121

    Cabbage Rolls, 118–19

    Cabbage Stew, 106

    Grilled Pork Chops, 110

    Lamb, Eggplant & Potato

        Casserole, 116–17

    Lamb, Leek & Potato

        Stew, 109

    Meat Pie, 128

    Meat Stew with

        Vegetables, 122

    Pork Rib & Lima Bean

        Stew, 114

    Roasted Leg of Lamb, 124

    Roasted Pork with

        Sauerkraut & Rice, 126

    Stuffed Peppers, 112

mushrooms

    Chicken &

        Mushrooms, 154

nuts

    Almond Cookies, 245

    Filo & Walnut Pastry

        (Baklava), 231

    Garlic & Walnut Dip, 32

    Shredded Filo & Almond

        Pastry, 237

    Walnut Bread, 212

okra

    Veal & Okra Soup, 91

Olives, 24

onions

    Beef & Onion Stew, 121

pasta

    Chicken & Orzo, 142

pastry. *See* breads; sweets

Pear Strudel, 234

peppers, hot

    Pepper & Tomato

        Scrambled Eggs, 197

    Spicy Peppers, 23

peppers, sweet. *See* bell peppers

pork

    Cabbage Rolls, 118–19

    Cabbage Stew, 106

    Grilled Pork Chops, 110

    Grilled Sausage Skewers, 35

    Ground Meat Pastry

        Filling, 225

    Meat Pie, 128

    Meat Stew with

        Vegetables, 122

    Pork Rib & Lima Bean

        Stew, 114

    Pork & Rice Soup, 95

    Roasted Pork with

        Sauerkraut & Rice, 126

    Stuffed Grape Leaves, 42

potatoes

    Baked Fish & Potatoes, 170

    Fried Potatoes, 188

    Lamb, Eggplant & Potato

        Casserole, 116–17

    Lamb, Leek & Potato

        Stew, 109

    Potato Cakes, 192

    Potato Salad, 58

    Roasted Cornish Hens

with Cabbage &

    Potatoes, 150

    Roasted Potatoes, 178

poultry

    Baked Chicken with

        Vegetables, 153

    Braised Quail, 141

    Chicken &

        Mushrooms, 154

    Chicken & Orzo, 142

    Chicken Pie, 145

    Chicken & Rice, 146

    Chicken Skewers, 138

    Fried Skillet Chicken

        Breasts, 136

    Roasted Cornish Hens

        with Cabbage &

        Potatoes, 150

    Spiced Chicken, 135

    Stuffed Chicken with

        Leeks & Cheese, 148

preserves

    Cherry Preserves, 264

    Dried Tomatoes, 259

    Fig Jam, 261

    Pickled Vegetables, 257

    Plum Preserves, 262

    Yogurt, 266

Pumpkin Pastry Filling, 225

Quail, Braised, 141

rice

    Chicken & Rice, 146

    Chicken & Rice Soup

        with Egg & Lemon, 88

    Meatball & Rice Soup

        with Spinach, 84

    Pork & Rice Soup, 95

Rice Pilaf, 181

Rice Pudding, 242

Roasted Pork with

Sauerkraut & Rice, 126

rolls. *See* breads

salads

Beet Salad, 57

Cabbage Salad, 72

Carrot Salad, 71

Cucumber Salad, 63

Macedonian Mixed

Salad, 53

Potato Salad, 58

Roasted Eggplant Salad, 64

Roasted Sweet Pepper

Salad, 61

Summer Salad, 54

Watermelon Salad, 68

Wheat Berry Salad, 67

White Bean Salad, 75

sauerkraut

Roasted Pork with

Sauerkraut & Rice, 126

Sauerkraut Pastry

Filling, 224

Sausage Skewers,

Grilled, 35

sesame seeds

Sesame Cookies, 241

Sesame Rings, 216–17

small plates

Bite-Size Meatballs, 41

Fried Smelts, 44

Garlic & Walnut Dip, 32

Grilled Sausage

Skewers, 35

Leek Crêpes, 47

Olives, 24

Roasted Eggplant Dip, 29

Roasted Pepper & Feta

Cheese Dip, 38

Roasted Red Pepper &

Eggplant Dip, 27

Spicy Peppers, 23

Stuffed Grape Leaves, 42

Yogurt with Garlic,

Cucumber & Dill, 31

Zucchini Fritters, 37

Smelts, Fried, 44

soups. *See also* stews

Chicken & Rice Soup

with Egg & Lemon, 88

Chilled Cucumber Soup, 81

Fish Soup, 96

Lentil Soup, 87

Meatball & Rice Soup, 84

Pork & Rice Soup, 95

Split Pea Soup, 101

Tripe Soup, 98

Veal & Okra Soup, 91

Vegetable Soup, 92

White Kidney Bean

Soup, 83

Sour Cream Cake, 233

Spinach Pastry

Filling, 224

Split Pea Soup, 101

squash

Roasted Acorn Squash, 191

Squash Pastry Filling, 225

stews

Beef & Onion Stew 121

Cabbage Stew, 106

Lamb, Leek & Potato

Stew, 109

Meat Stew with

Vegetables, 122

Pork Rib & Lima Bean

Stew, 114

Traditional White Bean

Stew, 177

Summer Salad, 54

sweets

Almond Cookies, 245

Filo & Walnut Pastry

(Baklava), 231

Fritters, 238

Pear Strudel, 234

Rice Pudding, 242

Sesame Cookies, 241

Shredded Filo & Almond

Pastry, 237

Sour Cream Cake, 233

Syrup Cake, 248

Syrup Doughnuts, 251

Yogurt Cake, 247

tomatoes

Dried Tomatoes, 259

Pepper & Tomato

Scrambled Eggs, 197

Stewed Green Beans with

Tomatoes & Roasted

Red Peppers, 184

Tripe Soup, 98

veal

Meat Stew with

Vegetables, 122

Veal & Okra Soup, 91

vegetables & side dishes

Cabbage with Dill, 187

Fried Eggplants, 182

Fried Potatoes, 188

Pepper & Tomato

Scrambled Eggs, 197

Pickled Vegetables, 257

Potato Cakes, 192

Rice Pilaf, 181

Roasted Acorn Squash, 191

Roasted Potatoes, 178

Roasted Vegetables, 194

Stewed Green Beans with

Tomatoes & Roasted

Red Peppers, 184

Traditional White Bean

Stew, 177

Vegetable Soup, 92

Watermelon Salad, 68

Wheat Berry Salad, 67

yogurt, 266

Chilled Cucumber

Soup, 81

Yogurt Cake, 247

Yogurt with Garlic,

Cucumber & Dill, 31

Zucchini Fritters, 37

Bosnia &
Herzegovina

Montenegro

Adriatic Sea

Italy